THE SPIRITUAL FLOWER GARDEN

THE SPIRITUAL FLOWER GARDEN

Geistliches Blumengärtlein

The First Complete English Translation

Volume One

GERHARD TERSTEEGEN

(1697–1769)

Translated and Edited by
Jarred Fenlason, D.Min.

The Spiritual Flower Garden
Volume One

Originally by Gerhard Tersteegen
Geistliches Blumengärtlein inniger Seelen (1729)

English translation and editorial material
© 2026 Jarred Fenlason
Original German text is in the public domain.

All rights reserved. No part of this publication may be reproduced, distributed, or transmitted in any form or by any means without the prior written permission of the publisher, except in the case of brief quotations embodied in critical reviews and certain other noncommercial uses permitted by copyright law.

Scripture taken from the New King James Version ®.
Copyright © 1982 by Thomas Nelson. Used by permission. All rights reserved.

First Complete English Translation

Published by
Encounter Press
Charlotte, North Carolina
www.encounterpress.com

ISBN 979-8-9941752-4-8 (This Volume, Paperback)
ISBN 979-8-9941752-5-5 (This Volume, Hardcover)
ISBN 979-8-9941752-6-2 (Volume Two, Paperback)
ISBN 979-8-9941752-7-9 (Volume Two, Hardcover)
ISBN 979-8-9941752-3-1 (Complete Edition, Ebook)

ALSO BY JARRED FENLASON
The Interval: The Brief Window that Shapes Your Eternal Soul
Encounter Discipleship: An Interactive Biblical Discipleship Program

Printed in the United States of America
First Edition: 2026

To those still seeking the hidden way

Song of Solomon 1:7

— ༒ —

To dwell alone with You, Beloved,
Is blessedness on earth;
What the mad world offers
Can give me naught but trouble.
To dwell alone with You, Beloved,
Is blessedness on earth,
When we cleave to You alone
Beyond sense, and place, and time.
To dwell alone with You, Beloved,
Is blessedness on earth,
Until You shall wholly raise us
Into the rest of eternity.

— ༒ —

— Gerhard Tersteegen
Solitary Summer Delight (Hymn 67)

CONTENTS

A Word Before the Garden — xi
Tersteegen's Preface to the Reader — xxi

1. Book I — 1
   Short and Edifying Verse
2. Book II — 169
   Meditations and Spiritual Verses

Glossary of Key Terms — 281
About the Translator — 285
Also by Jarred Fenlason — 287

A WORD BEFORE THE GARDEN

I was not looking for Gerhard Tersteegen. I was looking for witnesses.

For years I had been drawn to the voices of those who seemed to have crossed some threshold the rest of us only glimpse—men and women who wrote not merely *about* God but *from* God, whose sentences carried the unmistakable weight of firsthand encounter. The mystics. The desert dwellers. The quiet ones who slipped beneath the surface of religion and touched something living. I collected their books the way some collect relics: handled them carefully, returned to them often, hoped something might transfer.

It was during one of these searches that I came upon a slim volume titled *The Quiet Way: A Christian Path to Inner Peace*, a selection of Tersteegen's writings translated by Emily Chisholm. I read it once and felt the familiar stir of recognition—here was another witness. I read it a second time, more slowly, and began to suspect I had found something rarer: a guide. By the third reading, I knew. This was not a man reporting on the spiritual life from a comfortable distance. This was a man who had been there, who had descended into the darkness and emerged with something to say about the light. His prose did not argue or perform. It simply spoke—with the calm authority of one who knows the terrain because he has walked it, often alone, often at great cost.

I wanted everything he had written.

What followed was a years-long pursuit through his letters, his hymns, his meditations. And it was there, in the accumulating pile of German texts, that I discovered the problem: the majority of Tersteegen's work had never been translated into English. His masterpiece, the *Geistliches Blumengärtlein*—a work that shaped German-speaking piety for three centuries—remained locked behind a language barrier, available only in fragments, quoted but never fully rendered. Nearly three hundred years after its first publication, this garden had no gate for English readers.

This translation is that gate.

I offer it not as a scholar of German but as a minister and pilgrim who recognized in Tersteegen's voice something the church still needs to hear. His promise to his own readers remains his promise to you: "May God lure you more and more out of yourself and all created things. May He lead you into the sweet wilderness of inner solitude, and there speak to your soul like a friend."

Enter the garden. He is waiting to speak.

The Hidden Life of Gerhard Tersteegen

A Brief Life of Gerhard Tersteegen (1697–1769)

Gerhard Tersteegen spent his life trying to vanish—and failed spectacularly.

He wanted solitude; crowds found him. He sought obscurity; his words crossed borders. He retreated to a cottage to weave ribbons in silence; people climbed ladders to his windows just to hear him speak. The quiet man from Mülheim became one of the most influential spiritual voices of eighteenth-century Europe—not by seeking influence, but by fleeing it. His story reads like a parable he might have written himself: the soul that loses itself finds more than it bargained for.

Born in 1697 in Mörs, a small town on the Lower Rhine, Gerhard was the seventh of eight children in a prosperous merchant family. His father died when he was six. The boy showed early promise in classical studies—Latin orations, Greek and Hebrew—and everyone assumed he would enter the ministry. His widowed mother had other plans. The family needed merchants, not more scholars. At fifteen, Gerhard was apprenticed to his brother-in-law's shop in Mülheim.

The teenager did not take easily to commerce. Dry goods and ledgers held no charm for a mind shaped by ancient languages. But Mülheim offered something his Latin books had not: a living tradition of Pietist devotion. Prayer meetings hummed through the town. Spiritual songs drifted from workshops. A tailor-turned-schoolmaster named Backhaus had been leading conventicles since the days of Labadie, and a new generation of seekers gathered in homes and barns to pursue what they called *inwardness*—a faith felt in the soul's Ground, not merely professed from the pulpit.

Gerhard was drawn in. Somewhere in those early years—perhaps through a near-death experience in Duisburg forest, perhaps through a dying clergyman's prayer—he resolved to give himself wholly to God. But the resolution proved easier to make than to keep. The rushing current of business life, he later wrote, was "too rapid for his frail barque." After two years of shopkeeping on his own, he quit. He tried weaving; his constitution couldn't bear it. Finally, in a small cottage on the edge of town, he settled into the quieter trade of ribbon-making—a vocation requiring only a silk-twister's occasional company and leaving ample room for prayer.

What followed was not the peaceful idyll he imagined. It was five years of spiritual darkness.

From 1719 to 1724, Tersteegen descended into what can only be called a prolonged crisis of the soul. Influenced by the Quietists and mystics he was reading—Madame Guyon, Jacob Böhme—he wrestled with questions of self-denial, grace, and the hiddenness of God. He stopped attending the Reformed Church, unable in conscience to commune alongside what he considered "open sinners." He ate once a day. His relatives, embarrassed by this peculiar ascetic in the family tree, refused to speak his name. When illness confined him to bed for weeks at a time, no one brought him water.

And then, on Maundy Thursday 1724, something broke open.

Tersteegen emerged from his long tunnel with an assurance of Christ's reconciling grace—not earned by his striving, but given. To mark the moment, he did something extraordinary: he wrote out a solemn covenant with God and signed it in his own blood. The document, renewed each Easter for the rest of his life, survives. It was not performance or morbidity; it was a tradesman's contract, drawn up with the materials at hand, sealing what words alone could not contain.

The poetry began immediately. Where the five dark years had produced silence, the years that followed produced a torrent: hymns, meditations, verses of compressed spiritual wisdom. In 1729, he published the first edition of *Geistliches Blumengärtlein*—a modest title for what would become one of the most beloved devotional works in the German language. John Wesley would translate several of its hymns into English. German congregations still sing them today.

But Tersteegen wanted to remain invisible. He declined a wealthy patron's invitation to visit King Frederick the Great. He refused formal ordination. He never founded a sect or denomination, insisting, "I am a universal Christian." His cottage, which he called *die Pilgerhütte*—the Pilgrim's Cottage—was meant to be a retreat, a hidden cell for prayer.

It became, instead, a destination.

Word spread. Pilgrims arrived—first a trickle, then a stream. They came from the Rhineland, from Holland, from Scandinavia. The cottage that accommodated eight soon overflowed. When Tersteegen preached, the lower rooms of his house filled with six hundred souls; latecomers propped ladders against the windows, straining to catch a few words from the prophet inside. A Dutch nobleman of high rank read Tersteegen's books, abandoned his position and wealth, and moved to Amsterdam to live a hidden life with God—then invited Tersteegen to visit. The visit became an annual pilgrimage in reverse: the man who had fled the world now traveling to minister to those who had fled it after him.

Why did they come? Not for eloquence or spectacle. Tersteegen was frail, often ill, and spoke with the plainness of a ribbon-weaver. But those who met him reported something harder to name: a presence. The atmosphere around him seemed charged with the God he spoke of. His correspondence was vast, his counsel patient, his prayers fervent. He also became, improbably, a lay physician—mixing medicines in a small apothecary's laboratory in his home, treating the poor without charge. "The physician of the poor and forsaken," they called him.

The Prussian authorities were less impressed. In 1740, a law against unauthorized religious gatherings forced Tersteegen underground for a decade. He ministered privately, wrote constantly, and waited. When the restrictions lifted in 1750, the crowds returned—larger than before.

He died on April 3, 1769, worn out by the service he had never sought. His final years were marked by weakness and unceasing visitors: the sick in body, the sick in soul, the curious, the desperate. Letters piled up unopened on his desk. A friend once found him drenched in cold sweat, surrounded by petitioners. "Tersteegen must not be spared," he said. "He must have no rest."

It was not a complaint. It was a kind of joy.

His house in Mülheim still stands, now a museum. The blood-signed covenant resides there. His *Blumengärtlein* ran through seven editions in his lifetime and countless more after. The hymns traveled farther than he ever did, crossing confessions and centuries.

Gerhard Tersteegen tried to disappear. But the God he served had other plans—plans that somehow always involve visibility for those who want none, and silence for those who clamor to be heard. He would have understood the irony. He might even have smiled.

"To be forgotten and despised," he once wrote, *"let this be your longing here on earth."*

It was the one prayer that went unanswered.

But the garden he planted remains.

The Shape of the Garden

The *Blumengärtlein* comprises three books and a final collection, each with its own character. Understanding their differences helps readers approach each rightly.

Book I contains 605 short and edifying verses—some only two lines, most under eight—meant to be plucked like flowers and pondered slowly. Tersteegen called them *Schlußreime*, "closing verses": compressed seeds of spiritual truth, pithy and direct, often startling in their simplicity.

Book II offers 120 meditations on the Prophets—Isaiah, Jeremiah, Ezekiel, and Daniel—each pairing a Scripture text with Tersteegen's poetic reflection. Following these are sixteen pieces on Christ's Ascension and forty-four poems translated by Tersteegen from the French mystic Madame Guyon, whose quiet spirituality Tersteegen admired and wished to share with German readers.

Book III gathers 122 hymns and devotions, including Tersteegen's most beloved—"Thou Hidden Love of God," "God Calling Yet," and "Lo, God Is Here" (*Gott ist gegenwärtig*). These are longer, formally structured pieces written for congregational singing or extended personal devotion. Many remain in German hymnals today.

The Devout Man's Lottery (*Die Frommen Lotterie*), which Tersteegen placed as a closing collection, presents 412 aphorisms—brief lots to be drawn at random for daily guidance, a practice common in Pietist circles. Each offers a morsel of wisdom, warning, or encouragement for the soul seeking God. Here they appear complete for the first time in English.

In total: over 1,300 individual pieces. Tersteegen arranged these deliberately, and this translation preserves his structure.

Translation Philosophy

I have adopted what I call a Moderate Pietist Style. This approach preserves Tersteegen's inward tone and theological precision without resorting to heavy archaism that can distance modern readers. The goal is devotional clarity without flattening the spiritual intensity of the original.

Where Tersteegen quotes or clearly echoes Scripture, I have followed the New King James Version. The NKJV preserves the dignity and cadence of the biblical idiom that shaped Tersteegen's world while rendering it in contemporary English. In places where Scripture is not directly cited but is strongly alluded to, I have translated as poetry while preserving a reverent resonance when the English naturally allows. Scripture references included in this volume reflect only those explicitly cited or clearly indicated in the original German text. All citations have been standardized to modern English book names and chapter–verse formatting for clarity and consistency.

Key terms from the German mystical vocabulary are rendered consistently throughout the volume. Words such as *Gelassenheit* (yieldedness), *Seelengrund* (Ground of the soul), *Verborgenheit* (hiddenness), and *Eigenwille* (self-will) carry substantial theological weight and recur frequently; careless variation would diminish their force. A translation concordance guided these decisions so that Tersteegen's conceptual world remains intact across the entire work.

For the hymns and devotional songs, my objective has been readable hymn poetry: English that is recognizably metrical and suitable for devotional reading, without forcing every line into strict tune-fitting.

About the Translation Process

Because this edition encompasses such varied material—brief aphorisms, extended hymns, prose meditations, and devotional poetry—the translation method was intentionally disciplined.

While I am not a scholar of the German language, this translation was produced with the assistance of advanced computational language tools—digital resources capable of rendering German text into English with remarkable accuracy. These tools functioned much as lexicons, concordances, and interlinear texts served scholars in earlier generations: they handled the mechanical labor of vocabulary and syntax, producing working drafts that I then shaped, tested, and refined. The technology has changed; the translator's task has not. The final translation reflects deliberate human judgment throughout—theological, poetical, devotional. The tools proposed; I decided.

Accuracy begins with the German text itself. The 1729 print edition (as preserved in facsimile) served as the canonical reference throughout. Where any discrepancy arose between working transcriptions and the original, the print reading governed.

To preserve consistency across more than 1,300 individual pieces, I developed and maintained a Translation Style Guide, a glossary of key terms, and a concordance mapping recurring German vocabulary to stable English equivalents. Words like *Gelassenheit*, *Seelengrund*, and *Eigenheit* appear dozens of times; without systematic control, their force would dissipate. These resources ensured that Tersteegen's conceptual world remains intact from the first poem to the last aphorism.

For the hymns and devotional songs, this meant preserving original stanza structures, aiming for consistent line lengths, and allowing rhyme to relax rather than padding theology to "make it rhyme." Lines that clunked at a steady pace were revised until they didn't.

A WORD BEFORE THE GARDEN

A Word to the Reader

This is not a book to be read quickly. Its strength lies in its stillness and its invitation to linger. Many of these hymns and meditations were written for believers seeking to quiet their souls before God; they yield more in meditation than in speed. Read slowly. Read prayerfully. Let the words descend into the interior places they speak of.

Some passages will feel immediate, others elusive. Do not hurry past the difficult lines. The spiritual life Tersteegen envisions is one of patient turning, gentle yielding, and steady recollection. Give the text time to work on you. Behind every exhortation lies his conviction that God Himself meets the humble and attentive soul.

All translation is imperfect, and no rendering can fully contain the grace of a life given wholly to God. I offer this work with gratitude—both for the spiritual heritage that formed Tersteegen and for the grace that continues to form us.

It is my prayer that these poems, hymns, and meditations lead you, as they have led many before you, into a deeper awareness of the hidden Love who seeks the surrendered heart.

May the stillness of Christ's presence meet you in these pages,
and may His Love draw you ever closer to the Ground of the soul.

— Jarred Fenlason, D.Min.
Charlotte, North Carolina
Epiphany 2026

TERSTEEGEN'S PREFACE TO THE READER

Gerhard Tersteegen
Mülheim an der Ruhr, May 10, 1768

1

Because I cannot know who today or tomorrow may take this book into their hands, I find it necessary to offer a brief word of explanation beforehand. Most of these rhymed meditations came to me unexpectedly, one here and one there, within a short time. Without thinking much of art or ornament, I simply set them on paper as they came into my thoughts.

I can therefore promise the reader nothing great from my little work, especially since it was written amid persistent headaches and bodily weakness. At first I had no intention of making these verses public; but some well-known friends, who had seen a few of them and expressed their benefit and approval, urged me to have them printed.

2

As for the subject matter itself—however poor or childish it may appear to a rational mind—it is nevertheless according to truth, indeed holy and divine. And if, through lack of light and wisdom, I have placed a word not as well as I ought, I gladly leave such matters to the judgment of an enlightened heart.

I have sought to express everything as clearly, simply, and with as few words as possible. For this reason I ask every reader to consider and reflect on these pages with quiet deliberation and attention.

3

If someone should not yet be able to grasp this or that, let him not be troubled; let him instead practice, together with me, the little he does understand and recognize as good. In due time the rest—and indeed much more—will become clear and useful.

Every Christian truth has its degrees and its proper season in which it is rightly understood. And it must be remembered that the best, most spiritual, and most divine truths—and above all the highest truth, which is God Himself—can never be rightly and certainly known except in and by a heart that has been made inward, spiritual, and still through the mortification of the flesh, the senses, the affections, the desires, and the will; and has been simplified and made childlike through the denial of the manifold workings and reasonings of the mind.

Where this disposition of heart is lacking, the soul is incapable of true divine illumination. All its knowledge and judgments about God and divine things remain weak and uncertain. And the more spiritual and divine a truth is, the more must a soul enter into this disposition in order to perceive it rightly and profitably.

4

One thing more I find highly necessary to mention. When I speak of a deep truth or of a pure state of the soul and use the word *I*, I speak only in the person of a soul that stands in such experience—not of myself, as though I actually possessed it. I have indeed recognized such truths in divine light by grace with sufficient certainty; yet this is very different from essential enjoyment, actual experience, and the possession of such a state.

It is with me as with a sick man who loves and longs for health and gladly hears of it, though he does not yet enjoy it. So also, at times, I write of very spiritual and inward truths—not as though I had already attained them, but because I recognize them through the grace of God as so precious and lovely that I embrace them with my heart and long to experience them, and cannot refrain from weakly commending them to others when occasion offers.

5

Ah, that so many hungry souls linger so long, contenting themselves with dry and powerless husks and shadow-images of the truth, in which the Spirit can find no lasting delight or peace; while the essential core truths of the inward Christian life—truths that may be experienced even here on the pilgrim way through God's grace—are, if not despised, at least so little known, enjoyed, and recognized in their beauty and preciousness that it cannot be lamented enough with compassion!

People search far and wide, with much effort, for a treasure they never truly find—though they could have it so easily and so near—if they would only, with God's assistance, enter into the proper readiness and disposition of heart.

6

Come, you souls called by God to His pure service in the Spirit! Let us, in the strength of the Lord, free ourselves—and be freed—from all that is visible, from the senses, from reason, and from all self-will, so that, as truly detached, simplified, and pure creatures, we may enter into our spirit and into the Ground of our soul, and there find God, who is Spirit; and thus behold Him, love Him, and enjoy His peace, which is higher than all reason.

7

If anyone finds in this little work something good for his edification and awakening in a childlike walk before God, let him consider that it is the Father of lights from whom every good gift—and therefore also these—comes down from above, and let him give all honor and thanks, together with me, to the true giver of this good.

As for me, I shall rejoice with all my heart if even a single soul—I will not say be converted, but only receive a small strengthening and awakening in its inward walk through God's working—should benefit from it. And in such a case I trust that such a soul will not refuse my earnest request to commend the one who has written these things, with a heartfelt sigh, to the Author and Finisher of faith.

8

The foregoing was written for the first edition of this little book. Since it has pleased God that it should be made known through the press, I have not hesitated in later editions to add various additional verses on the same subject as they came to hand—something I have done all the more willingly since I have seen, with humble gratitude, that the Lord has blessed this simple testimony of His truth in the hearts of many.

Through this I have been strengthened in the understanding that God, in His wondrous condescension, sometimes makes our small and fragile efforts worthy of His blessing, so that we do not remain fixed upon any means or instrument, but look to Him alone and allow ourselves to be drawn to Him—so that we may drink the waters of life fresh from the fountain, which so gladly spring up in our dry Ground of soul and desire to impart themselves richly to each of us.

9

Ah yes, you thirsty and weary hearts, let this be reminded to you once more in God's name, and receive it in simple faith as the priceless kernel of the true Gospel: that to us—utterly corrupted by nature and held fast under the power of darkness—the gentle, ever-welling love of God has been opened again in the Ground of our heart in the gracious and lovely name Jesus Immanuel, and has become unspeakably near, though because of our estrangement, inner darkness, and confusion, we cannot always perceive it clearly.

Since the kingdom of God has come so near—indeed inwardly into us —we need no longer make any long detour through much knowing or our own workings, but through this opened new and living way (Heb. 10:20) may go straight into the sanctuary of intimate and eternal communion with God.

We need only let ourselves be led by the faithful discipline, drawing, and power of this deeply hidden, near love of God out of all deceitful pleasures of the world and the tormenting life of Self-hood, giving our heart and will so bare and blind into the captivity of this inward love that it may be our all in all and lead us as it pleases.

Behold, this is the whole matter. Then one remains and becomes ever more a simple little child of heart, practicing freely without artifice in abiding, loving, suffering, and yielding; and thus, purely by grace, becomes righteous, holy, and blessed from now on, and has fellowship with the Father in His Son Jesus Christ. Amen.

"And now, little children, remain in Him, so that when He is revealed we may have confidence and not be put to shame before Him at His coming" (1 John 2:28).

10

Closing Prayer

> Draw me until my all is brought into You,
> O mighty Magnet who touches my deepest ground
> with Your Godhead-love,
> that through hidden impulse
> the Spirit's hunger eternally
> may rest in nothing that You are not.
> It is far too narrow for him; he must have You Yourself.
> In Your own element must he satisfy his hunger.
> Draw me out of myself and all creation—
> cost what it may, draw me, draw me still.
> Let all bonds be torn
> until I blessedly come to rest
> in You, the harbor of my peace.
> There I shall close my joyful eyes;

TERSTEEGEN'S PREFACE TO THE READER

there hunger, thirst, and striving cease,
for I can embrace You Yourself
in the Ground of the soul.
My will lies there broken and yielded,
my mouth is silent in reverence,
my spirit bows inwardly
and nestles at Your feet as Yours,
and then it knows the meaning of this word:
I am content.

Closing Verses
The little flowers stand here,
planted upon the paper.
May God Himself paint them,
water them, and shine upon them;
may the heart be their soil,
and may each little flower
become truth, power, and substance
in all who read them.

BOOK I
SHORT AND EDIFYING VERSE

BOOK I

Translator's Note: The first ten entries appear in both German and English to demonstrate the translation method employed throughout. From Poem 11 onward, the English stands alone.

Readers will encounter one term that lacks a clear contemporary equivalent: "Ground" or "Ground of the soul" (German: Seelengrund). Derived from the medieval mystic Meister Eckhart, it names the deepest point of the soul where it meets God—a place untouched by creatureliness, beneath thought and feeling. Tersteegen constantly urges readers to "turn inward" and "sink into the Ground" where God waits. The word is capitalized throughout this translation to signal its technical, doctrinal meaning. A Glossary at the end of this volume defines this and other key terms from the Rhenish mystical tradition.

These verses reward unhurried reading.

1. An den Leser

Mensch, Gott dein Anfang ist; hast du ihn selbst im Wesen,
So hast du schon das End' von dieser Schrift gelesen.
Suchst du ihn noch, so lies dies auf der Pilgerbahn!
Bist du ein solcher nicht, so geht es dich nicht an.

To the Reader

O man, God is your origin; if you have Him in your very
  being,
Then you have already read the end of all that stands herein.
If still you seek Him, then read this on your pilgrim way;
But if you are not such a one, this book concerns you not
  today.

2. Wo der Schatz ist, da ist das Herz

Wenn Herz und Sinn und Lust so gerne auswärts fliegen,
So hat man Gott noch nicht, so lebt man jämmerlich.
Wer Gott im Grund besitzt, der läßt sich wohl begnügen
Mit diesem einen Gut; drum kehrt er stets in sich.

Where the Treasure Is, There the Heart Is

When heart and mind and longing still so gladly stray abroad,
It shows one has not God, and lives a sorry life.
But he who holds God in the Ground is quietly sufficed
With this one only Good, and turns within again.

3. Geduldig sein in Kreuz und Pein

Senk dich fein tief in Gottes Lieb' hinein,
Dann kannst du leicht sanft, still, gelassen sein!
Des Herren Kreuz ist solch ein sanftes Kissen,
Man sollt' es nicht für Seid' und Sammet missen.

Be Patient in Cross and Pain

Sink but deep into the love of God,
Then may you gently, still, and yielded be.
The Lord's own Cross is such a tender pillow—
One would not trade it for silk or velvet fine.

4. Anbetung im Geist

»Ich bet' dich an, mein Gott«, ein andrer öfters spricht;
Mein Geist es immer tut, doch sagt mein Mund es nicht.

Adoration in the Spirit

"Lord, I adore You," many another says;
My spirit ever does—though not my mouth always.

5. Wie Gott gesucht werde

Laß los die Kreatur, entsink dem eignen Willen,
Gedenk nicht mehr an dich und laß dich Gott im Grund
Demütig, liebreich, sanft, merk, wenn er dich will stillen;
So findst du dich in Gott und Gott in dir zur Stund'!

How God Is to Be Sought

Let go the creature-things, let fall your own self-will;
Think not upon yourself, but yield to God within—
Humble, gentle, loving—mark when He would still you;
So find yourself in God, and God in you that hour.

6. Ost, West; zu Haus ist's best'

Mein Geist gehört in Gott zu Haus,
Drum kehrt er sich aus allem aus;
Sein Vaterland heißt Ewigkeit,
Drein senkt er sich aus Ort und Zeit,
Da er im innig stillen Nun
In Gott kann im Verborg'nen ruhn.

East, West; at Home Is Best

> My spirit's home is God alone;
> Therefore it turns from all things else.
> Its fatherland is called Eternity;
> Into that realm it sinks from time and place,
> There, in the inward, silent Now,
> It may in God, the hidden One, find rest.

7. Jesus zu der Seele

> *Ei, stör dich nicht, mein Kind, bleib innig abgeschieden*
> *In sanft und stillem Geist, in unverrücktem Sinn;*
> *Laß kommen, was da will, bewahre deinen Frieden,*
> *Nichts ist des Störens wert, Ich, Jesus, in dir bin;*
> *Hab Ruh in mir, daß ich in dir kann ruhn,*
> *Was will dir Welt und alle Teufel tun!*

Jesus to the Soul

> Ah, be not troubled, child; remain withdrawn within,
> In gentle, quiet spirit and in steadfast mind.
> Let come whatever may—yet guard your peace;
> No thing is worth disturbance, for I, Jesus, am in you.
> Rest in Me, that I may rest in you;
> What can the world or all its devils do to you?

8. Jesus zu der Seele

> *Du sprichst, ich möge dich bewirken und bereiten;*
> *Nun, streck die Hände aus und laß mich machen dann!*
> *Dein eig'ner Will' und Sorg', dein Treiben und Arbeiten*
> *Stört deine Ruh und macht, daß ich nicht wirken kann.*

Schau nur die Blümlein an bei heiterm Sommerwetter,
Sie halten sich ganz still und öffnen ihre Blätter,
So scheint die Sonne drein und wirket sänftiglich;
So will ich's machen auch, halt dich nur leidentlich!

Jesus to the Soul

You say you would prepare your heart for Me;
Then stretch your hands to Me and let Me work therein.
Your own will, care, and striving—these disturb your rest
And hinder Me from working as I would.
Behold the little flowers on a clear summer day:
They stand entirely still and open wide their leaves;
So shines the sun upon them, working gently.
Thus would I work in you—only be still and consenting.

9. Wie man leicht Gott erreicht

Nur die Lust von allem scheiden,
Wenig tun und vieles leiden,
Lieben, still und fröhlich sein,
Macht das Herz mit Gott gemein.

How One Easily Reaches God

Only part from every earthly pleasure,
Do but little, suffer much,
Love, be still, be quietly joyful—
So is the heart made one with God.

10. Wie man Gott findet

Gedenk nicht weit hinaus, willst du Gott in dir finden;
Was ist und wird geschehn, laß alles sanft verschwinden
Und bleibe wie ein Kind ohn' Sorg', ohn' Witz und Will'!
Es braucht nicht große Kunst, Gott wohnet in der Still'.

How One Finds God

Think not afar, if you would find God in you;
Let what is and what shall be gently fade away,
And stay as does a child—without its care or wit or will.
No art is needed here; God dwells in the stillness.

11. Jesus' Eye and Heart Ease Pain and Grief

The best of medicines in every grief and pain:
The eye upon the Cross of Christ, His great glory;
The will in Jesus' hand, the love in Jesus' heart;
The head upon His lap—this eases every sorrow.

12. The Best Use of Time

Lose yourself with world and time,
Sink deeply into eternity—
So have you, verily, day and night,
Spent all your hours in the very best way.

13. The Single Eye

Would you behold God truly with the eyes of spirit?
Then look on Him alone—and soon it shall be so.
You look now at this, now at that—
Are here and then are there;
But Godhead is but One, and in your Ground is near.

14. Jesus to the Soul

Child, would you rightly grasp Me?
Then must you yield yourself to Me.
Who leaves himself and all things else
Has Me in everlasting hold.

15. The Most Glorious Shortening of Time

If time seems long already to the people of this age,
How long to them shall that long Eternity appear!
But I—even when I sit in stillness—have ever much to do;
Eternity seems short to him who rests in God.

16. The Greatest Unmercifulness

When you seek content in self or creature,
Your poor spirit—believe it—cannot breathe.
O unmerciful one to your own soul, give it air!
God is its element, who kindly calls to you.

17. Doing No More Is the Best Repentance

O Jesus, Mother-heart, so faithful and so true;
Though I run far from You, You draw me back again.
Let this not happen more—hold fast Your own possession
That lays itself, O Love, upon Your breast.

18. What Sweetly Fragrants, Quickly Flees

If one is once delighted by the Lord,
And kindly looked upon within the Ground,
And others praise and chatter much of this—
Thereafter must one stand in drought.
The love that no one knows of
Is the happiest state of love.

19. The Best Company

Go, creatures, go—I can forego you all!
My truest Friend remains, so inwardly near.
I turn into my chamber and shut fast the door
To keep company there with my soul's dear Friend.
When I am thus alone from all created things,
I am the more in fellowship with the Creator.

20. O That I Were So!

Small, and pure, and set apart,
Gentle, simple, still, at peace—
Will-less, inwardly full of joy;
Ah, would my soul but be so!

21. Jesus to the Soul

My child, why do you wander so with heart and mind and thought?
Is My own presence then to you no longer known?
And can I not give your spirit truer satisfaction
Than all creation with its false delight?

22. Jesus to the Soul

Run not without Me; you will stumble, err to either side.
You are a feeble child; your doing has no understanding.
Therefore, where you go and where you stand,
Let yourself be led by Me—cling closely to My hand!

23. Stay at Home!

You urge God so often—yet are ever running out;
And when He comes to visit you, you are not home.

24. The Best Study

Another strives in learning, reading, endless study,
Longing to be great, longing to do great things.
My task is this: to forget and lose all things,
To become nothing in myself, and rest in God.

25. What Is Our Work?

He who does God's will and bears God's will,
Who parts his heart's delight from every earthly thing,
Who yields his will entirely to God's power—
Though he should do no more, his work is fully done.

26. If You Can Do Nothing, You Must Rest

If you can do but little, then be still and suffer;
And what is best omitted, avoid it where you can.
Wait on the Lord in patience! If you can rest in Him,
He will Himself accomplish all in you and through you.

27. Where Is God?

Reason says, 'Where is God?' and gazes at the stars.
'Where is the sun?' says one born blind.
Ah, become a child, and God is near indeed—
Turn inward with your sight, the spirit sees Him there!

28. All in God's Name

Would you take something up? Then lay your heart beforehand
Indifferent, quiet, bare before God's shining light.
Hold back your own impulse—it brings but harm and sorrow!
Do your work in God, and yoau need fear no thing.

29. At Home It Will Go Better

Ah pilgrim, faint not—hold out a little longer,
And keep yourself withdrawn from all that soon must vanish.
Time shortens evermore; you shall be home anon,
Where you shall find with your Father all you have desired.

30. Self-Denial Better Than Gifts

Revelation, gifts of wonder,
Comforts, sweetnesses in prayer,
Despising honor, world, and riches,
Knowing much and pondering more,
Fasting, reading, singing, praying,
Speaking with the tongue of angels—
None of this I count as gain
Where the will is not subdued.

31. Each Has Something He Loves

Each one has something that he loves,
Each one has something that keeps him company,
Each one has something that shortens time,
Each one has something that gives delight,
Each one has something he leans upon and trusts,
Each one has something he loves to gaze upon.
What then shall I choose? O Jesus, You alone—
Be You my treasure, good, my comfort, all in all!

32. True Yieldedness

Now one follows not God at all; now another runs too fast.
One is far too sluggish; another over-busy.
Lord, were I but toward You as is my hand,
Methinks I then would hold the perfect middle way.

33. Going Out Was Never So Good; Staying In Is Better

Another goes abroad and loves his diversions;
I go within, and so I am not led astray.
And when I must go out, I still remain turned inward,
That even in my going I am not drawn away.

34. Jesus to the Soul

Am I not enough for you? Why wander all your senses?
The creature deceives—its beauty is but show.
What you seek outwardly, you find here within;
Would you love Me aright? Then love Me only.

35. How One Defends Oneself

I am a helpless child, bereft of wit and strength,
While thousands stand against my soul.
O Jesus, Mother-heart, I creep into Your breast
And will not stir, though all the world should fall.

36. Seldom Does It Suit Us

Always you have something in your head;
Always you have something to be done.
Though God Himself draw near to you,
He finds no rest with you.

37. God Must Also Speak

You have so many things to say to God—
Now you would have this, now you come to complain of that.
Give Him some room—be silent for a little while,
And mark what He would say and what He asks of you!

38. Self-Pleasing

What God bestows, receive; yet take not pride in it—
Else you will do the very thing that Lucifer has done.

39. The Human Spirit

A spirit—wondrous thing! Though it should gain
All earth and heaven hold, it would not be content.
But when it finds God deep within the Ground,
Though it possess naught else, it says, 'I am satisfied.'

40. Everything in Its Right Place

A stone inclines toward earth;
A little flame climbs upward;
A fish must live within the water;
A bird must hover in the air.
When each is where it should be,
It rests, and all is well.
My spirit is quiet and content
When it lies in God, its point of rest.

41. From the Head into the Heart

God is a God of the heart; therefore, if you would find Him,
Blind your reason—for it will never fathom Him.
Sink down from all your thinking into the Ground of the
    heart,
Gently, lovingly, as a child—and He will meet you there.

42. Like Meets Like; Like Finds Like

God is simplicity itself—gentle, pure, withdrawn,
Unbounded, quiet, ever joyful, ever still.
Strive to become so in your inmost Ground,
And God and all His truth shall soon be known to you.

43. He Who Begins Aright Is Half Done

You say it is hard to force your lust, your mind, your will.
Yes, force is painful—but begin the work with God,
And soon with gladness you shall lightly do
What once, by your own effort, you did force in vain.

44. The Lord Is in This Place

God is ever near you; God is ever mindful of you.
He turns toward you and draws you toward Himself.
Mark, O soul, what I say, and let your heart and thinking
Be ever drawn by His pull of love toward Him.

45. You Must Be Exact and Pure

You are to be on earth
A temple of the Godhead.
How pure, O soul—how pure
Must then your heart become!
Desires and thoughts—hold them
In careful bounds and order,
And wait upon God's guard
As does a priest of old.

46. God and His Will Bring Stillness

He who desires nothing but God and God's dear will
Can quiet himself best in every circumstance.
Let come what may—he has what he desires;
Who longs for more but multiplies his grief.

47. Experience Makes One Wise

The disciples once were filled with the Holy Ghost.
I speculate not how this may be grasped.
Would I but see my heart made empty of myself and all things,
Soon would I happily experience and understand it.

48. How Strong the Enemy Is

My foe is strong—or weak—according as I look.
If I see only him and me, he seems both great and strong;
But if I look to Jesus too, I scarcely heed him;
And if he seek to seize me, I crawl into Jesus' breast.

49. In Many Trials

To will nothing and to do nothing,
Only suffer, hope, and rest—
These best can calm
Temptation, trial, strife.

50. The Image of a Mirror

O would my heart be still and free of every spot,
Well polished through its sufferings like a mirror bright!
How sweetly would the sun of Godhead shine in me,
How soon would He paint His image in my Ground!

51. With God Alone in the World

Only God and I alone!—
So live on earth below,
If you would quickly, easily
Become right truly devout.

52. In the Dark, Close Your Eyes

When you are in the dark, do not turn round and round;
The narrow way to heaven oft runs strangely crooked.
He who will probe all things but loses himself in riddles—
A blind and simple soul cannot go wrong on this path.

53. The Wisest Physician

Ah, yield yourself to God; He is so wise and faithful.
Your poison of sin He uses as medicine.
But he who hides his sin beneath such grace as this
Shall find the draught he drinks most sour and bitter.

54. I, Too, Am Something Great

God is Himself my Father; I am the Bride of the Son;
His Spirit is the pledge and bond by which I'm given to Him.
God has bestowed on me more gift than all the seraphim;
The angels evermore attend and wait on me.
I have what I desire; the whole wide world is mine;
Hell is afraid of me; I fear my God alone.
In heaven I walk as one that is a queen—
Say, poor child of this world, am I not something great?

55. Children's Wills Must Be Broken

Follow not nature nor your fleshly will;
They are like little children, never satisfied.
They can be calmed no better than by self-denial;
If you are soft with them, you but increase all your pain.

56. Without Pretence

Do all things plain and right; never dissemble;
You deal with God, who sees into your heart.

57. Childlike and Trustful

God loves to make Himself familiar;
You must not be too shy.
Trustful, childlike, bare,
Sink into the Father's breast.
He, as your truest Friend,
Does mean you well indeed.

58. I Let God Alone Come In

The human heart must be a mighty thing:
God, devil, world, and flesh, and all, would enter there.
Since you can choose, then choose the noblest Guest;
If you have chosen what is good, hold fast what you have gained.

59. Dependence Brings Holiness

God is the sun; I am a little ray of light.
If I depart from Him, I am a darkened nothing.
But if I cleave to Him, then light and life are mine,
And all the virtues flow as His still influence.

60. Jesus to the Soul

Deny yourself, My child; you give Me delight.
Remember who I am—would you refuse Me this?

61. The Cause of All My Pain

All my pain springs forth from pride and self-willed ways,
Because I am no quiet child, surrendered unto God.

62. The Stranger Has No Concern

I am a pilgrim here; therefore it is not mine
To trouble for the deeds that others do in this strange world.

63. To a Rationalist

Reason-Christian, become a child at last,
Lay down your clever thoughts of head and mind.
Deny yourself and everything beside,
And bring your heart and will to God,
And walk before His face;
Your speculations cannot do this work.

64. Through Nothingness Goes the Way

O Christian, you would ever much possess and be and have;
Your Savior loved contempt, want, poverty, and pain.
Do the same! The path of peace and light—
Mark well my word—goes through the nothing, nothing,
    nothing.

65. Praise and Contempt

He who praises you but puts you to the test;
Remember, all men lie—be not deceived by them.
But he who holds you cheap does help you and does serve
The one who with Christ gladly would be hid in God.

66. A Christian's Threefold Occupation

He who loves God most purely is like a seraphim;
He who beholds Him in the spirit acts as a cherubim.
He who rests in God and lets God rest in him
Is not a sluggard—he does what all the heavenly thrones are
    doing.

67. I Have No Time

God is forever near. To die to self and live to Him,
To cleave with all my love to Him in stillest Ground—
This is my mighty work; I have no time to spare
To scatter me abroad and busy with other things.

68. If You Begin, Think Then Too

'My Lord, this would I do; I think it is Your will.
If You will have it not, behold, I let it go.
Whether it fail or thrive, I will remain at rest;
If You are but content, my work is fully done.'

69. In Jesus Alone You Find Rest

Yes, Jesus, it is true: the world is full of anguish;
As soon as I turn outward, my spirit is distressed.
So I return once more into You, my little chamber,
That, wholly set apart, I may enjoy Your peace.

70. Take Good Courage!

O soul, take courage now—what profit is your grieving?
God asks not very much: but love, and love, and love.
You say, 'I am so bad'; I answer, 'God is good.'
Cast yourself into Him—O soul, take courage now!

71. All or Not at All

Ah, do not split your heart; give all of it to God,
And lead your love entirely into Him alone.
Your little heart yet holds too small a love
To love an infinite Good as it is meet.

72. God's Goodness Draws to Repentance

You God of love, so good, so kind, so full of grace!
It might not seem so safe if bold sinners truly knew it.
Yet yes, it would be good, if he but left his life of sin;
His heart would surely break and yield to such a God.

73. A Quiet Life God Has Chosen

Jesus is a King of peace;
See, then—hear and speak but little;
What you do, do with thought,
Softly, gently, without stirring.
And in your every work
Keep watch on Him within,
That His throne of peace and realm
Depart not from your heart.

74. Let Nothing In; It Brings But Pain

The heart clings light and soft to every creature-thing;
But it is pain and strife before we let them go again.
So clasp with pleasure naught in heaven or on earth
Save what can nevermore be taken from you.

75. Who Loses, Finds

Where you find yourself, there must you lose yourself,
And bring all lust and love into God alone.
The truer you lose, the more you ever gain;
And when you are most poor, in God you find wealth.

76. All Eyes Are on You

God, angels, devil, world, and all are looking unto you;
Therefore live in holy fear and cling to God within.

77. Jesus to the Soul

O soul, leave off your worrying—this is My concern.
If you will worry too, then I will cease from care.
So stay hid in Me, sink deep into My breast,
And think no more upon yourself.

78. Living According to Your Station

Think, soul, that you are bride of the King of heaven,
Who chose you out from thousands and gave Himself to you.
Live worthy of such call; your heart is wholly His—
Let not your powers of love incline to creature-things.

79. The God-Surrendered Will Is Strong

Your deepest will must yield itself to God, not half but whole;
So can you stand against the whole fierce might of sin.

80. Take All from God's Hand

You deal but with God, whatever may befall;
You must not fix your eye on creatures or on outward things.
What means God uses here concerns you not at all;
Whatever meets you in the world—still think, 'My God has
    done it.'

81. On Solitude

If you would live by your own sense, however fair it seem,
Then solitude can never give you stillness.
He who departs from self can always be alone,
Content and undisturbed, even in the midst of men.

82. The Lamb's Image

O that I were like a lamb—
Innocent, gentle, pure, and patient!
O that men might read Christ's image,
Christ's own life and way,
In all my walk and bearing!

83. Complete Indifference

Like as a little leaf floats lightly in the air,
So even-poised my will-less mind in God's free breath does move.
No other wanting lives in me but God's own will;
His slightest sign blows all my will away—
To do or to forbear, to suffer or to rest,
To me 'tis all the same, Lord, if Your will be done.

84. For Fire and Flame, Water Is Good

When pride and lust and wrath and selfhood trouble you,
You must turn inward soon into God's love.
So shall the roaring power of evil pass away,
And soon your proud and stubborn mind grows gentle, soft, and small.

85. Dealing with People

In work and word and way
Be gentle, gracious everywhere
With all your fellow-men.
Yet, all the while, cleave inward
To God within your Ground,
As though you were alone.

86. The Self-Eye and the Single Eye

If in self-seeking you do secretly hunt yourself,
You shall in darkness dwell, in fear and restlessness.
But when your eye is single and seeks God alone,
You can in spirit live at peace and in the light.

87. He Who Has It Within Needs Not Run Out

I dare not turn me outward,
For I myself have in my house
The fountain that can fully satisfy.
I can well do without you, creature;
I turn into my Ground alone,
Where I may have my God Himself.

88. The Hidden Life

Live hidden in your God in holy separation,
A stranger and as dead unto the world and self.
Self-nature brings but pain—lose it, forget it quite!
Let no life be in you save Christ made manifest.

89. The Divine Moment

Sink into the quiet Now—the little point of time with God—
Softly, lovingly, nor look back nor on before.
Yield wholly up to Him, bow inward into Him,
And wait in patientness till He reveal Himself.

90. Lowly, Yet Confident

In yourself weak, small, and bare,
In God's strength mighty, great;
In deepest lowliness bowed down,
In faith unmoved and firm;
In spirit bold and free,
So walk day by day.

91. Jesus to the Soul

Still you go in yourself, your burdens on your back;
And I am ever near—can you not tell Me all?
Would you help yourself, poor creature that you are?
I gladly help you so—only be openhearted!

92. Christ's Blood Is Good for All

It is Christ's blood alone that reconciles my sin;
This tincture of His love breaks wrath's fierce power,
Revives my spirit, which else must burn in fire,
Makes fresh again what old and dead it finds.
Yet if it is to still me in my fear and need,
The fountain must spring up within my heart.

93. Bowed Beneath All Men

O soul, lay yourself always
In humble mind
At every person's feet.
If any wrong be done to you,
Receive it without murmur.
Whoever still thinks much of self
Before God—ah, misery!—does stink indeed.
If any good be seen in you,
Remember, it is God's—
It is but what He gave.

94. O That I Were Thus!

Free from love of creatures,
Dead to self-will's urge,
Much silence, inward, outward,
Still bending sweetly into God,
In fellowship with Him as does a child—
Blessed is he who ever thus can be!

95. You Must Live by Providence

The soul that has in truth
Given itself to God
As does a little child
Must live by providence.
Wait from moment unto moment
What God gives, takes, and does
For body and for soul—
He knows what profits you.

96. Meekness Quenches Hell's Fire

Jesus, by yielded love,
Turned back the Father's wrath
And hell's own raging fury.
If now His Spirit flow through you,
You too by love shall sweeten
All men's bitterness.

97. Jesus to the Soul

Child, close your eyes against this circling world;
Leave world to deal with world and all its painted toys.
Do but stay near Me within your soul's deep Ground,
And we shall walk together there in inward nearness.
What is the world to you? You soon shall leave it all;
Then we shall ever stay together in My Father's house.

98. One Thing Is Needful

Men seek full many things yet never are content;
But I am satisfied, for I seek only one.
They have much work to do; I have but one sole task—
To mark, in quietness, what Jesus says to me.

99. All for All

O soul, you must make over unto God
Your willing, loving, thinking,
And all you are and have, to be His own forever.
Go thoroughly out of self
And inward into Him,
So shall you ever be
The play of His delight.

100. True Freedom

Who seeks true liberty must press and bind
His flesh and senses and all selfhood round with narrow bands.
The freedom of mere nature but imprisons still the spirit;
Go out of self into your God if you would truly free.

101. Lord, As You Will!

Lord, as You will—this or that I do not choose;
Lord, as You will—only let it come to pass.
I am Your servant, my King—command only!
I will, as a child, look to You for every sign.

102. He Who Flees the Many Sees the One

In multiplicity you will not find the One;
Turn your eye from all things—let it be set inward.
And if you can forget and lose even yourself,
Soon shall you feel God in you—the true One.

103. Outer and Inner Stillness

How sweet it is when thoughts and limbs and senses,
Affections, will, and all desires are stilled;
When all is silent, outwardly and inwardly,
And in the clear Ground God is found present!

104. How One Obtains Peace

He who desires peace must break his will;
Else neither God nor all the heavens can quiet him.

105. He Who Truly Rests Does Much

Through self-will, action, striving,
You ever remain the same.
But he who lies withdrawn, will-less,
Yielded in God's bosom,
And rests from his own works,
Does before God the best of all works.

106. Where Is Heaven?

Ask not where heaven is—leave selfhood behind,
Else heaven remains far and strange wherever you are.
He who dies to his will and yields himself to God
Already lives with God in heaven upon the earth.

107. Where Is the Treasure Found?

Men seek and do not find, though the treasure is so near.
Why run about so much? It lies within the heart.
Sell only what you have and enter into yourself—
So shall the greatest treasure, God Himself, be yours.

108. Never Alone

Wherever I go or stand, or sit or work,
I am not alone—my Friend stands by my side.
If I remain close to Him and do what pleases Him,
He walks with me and gladly abides with me.

109. The Temple of Baal

Let nothing beside God enter into your Ground,
Else your heart, O man, becomes a temple of Baal.

110. Two Alone Make Fellowship

The more I remain alone with Jesus,
The more He makes Himself my companion.
When He and I alone are
In my heart's little chamber,
I have in Him deep peace;
Therefore I gladly remain withdrawn.

111. Give Me, My Child, Your Heart

God is so rich, yet still desires my gifts;
He gives Himself—should I then be so sparing?
My dearest and my best He ought to have;
My whole heart must be consecrated to Him.

112. Hold Nothing Back!

Give your beloved Benjamin
Willingly into God's hands;
Else fear remains within your soul,
And you must ever suffer inward torment.

113. Take Not to Heart What Is Done

If men hate you or love you,
If they take from you or give to you,
If they scold you or honor you,
And whatever else may happen—
Remain undisturbed and withdrawn,
Content with God within your Ground.

114. Obedience Is Better Than Sacrifice

He serves and loves God more
Who breaks his will,
Than he who does great works
According to his own design.

115. One Must Still Keep the Sabbath

In Sabbath-rest, in holy idleness,
You shall gain very much.
Let self-working cease,
And suffer God inwardly.
Be still in thought and will and desire;
Do not work much with head and heart.
Let time and place and everything be,
And even yourself, in truth.
Lose yourself quietly into the dark—
There dwells God's clarity.
If you can thus rest yielded in God,
What can hell's power do to you?

116. The Way Home

Keep ever your end in sight! It hinders your journey,
O pilgrim, if you look too much here and there.
Mark well how you must travel: out of yourself and all things,
With all your love—this is the way home.

117. Serving God in His Way

You must not serve God as you deem good.
He serves God who yields himself and does God's will.
And if one cannot do it, one can still suffer it;
He who wills nothing but God serves Him in both.

118. Do Not Leave Your Post!

Leave not your post! Let neither heart nor thoughts
Wander outward from their proper watch.
Stand guard always at the door of the heart.
You must not force your way in selfhood,
But wait in stillness, turned from all things,
Until you are admitted to the inner chamber.

119. Trust—and Let Yourself Be Led

You must venture blindly upon God,
Not ever searching, fearing, lamenting.
Yield yourself wholly in simplicity;
Lose yourself into God's hands.
As He leads you, so follow,
And ask not: 'Where does this go?'

120. Be Still—God Will Fight

When the enemy assaults you, do not be afraid;
Remain within the fortress—God Himself will guard you.
Despise the foe with courage and remain still in God;
He can do nothing to him who himself does nothing and wills nothing.

121. Boldly Dared Is Half Won

    Fear and constraint and timidity
    Hold the heart in anxious bondage;
    Then everything seems heavy.
    But love and joy and holy courage
    With God accomplish mighty deeds
    And set the spirit free.

122. Remember Lot's Wife

    Be steadfast—steadfast—
    Without looking back or turning aside;
    With heart and mind toward God alone,
    If you would reach the treasure.

123. He Who Loses His Life Shall Find It

    Do not fear when all supports are taken from you
    And you must hang exposed and bare.
    Lose yourself in the ocean of the Godhead;
    The deepest death brings you the purest life.
    Let all things go and close your eyes.
    If you do not lose, you shall never find.
    He who sinks from self finds rest in God;
    His true life remains—his own must disappear.

124. First Come—Then See

    God dwells beyond all time and place,
    Far from creatures and the senses,
    Still within Himself, in gentle peace.

If you would see Him, faithful Christian,
You must come where He is
And become likewise withdrawn.

125. Rest in None but God

Forsake creaturely comfort, and you shall gain God's gifts;
Yet rest not even in these, if you would have God Himself.

126. Stillness at the Center

The world is but a wheel, ever turning round;
If you enter it with desire, you are drawn into its motion.
God is the center—return into the Ground of the soul.
He who is gathered there can remain still and at peace.

127. Household Matters Do Not Concern the Infant

How foolish is the child who might rest in the bosom
Yet would worry and do great things himself!
He who is wise remains hidden in Jesus' breast,
Drinking grace upon grace while the Mother cares.

128. A Spiritual Voyage

My journey runs against the stream—what shall I do?
I am so faint and weary that I cannot row.
Here I sit still and wait, holding up the sails,
Until a favorable wind carries me along.

129. The Way of Blind Love

Blind love does not consider
That it itself lacks strength;
It knows that God can do all things.
Blind love does not weigh
What refreshes or what wounds;
It looks only upon God.
Blind love does not wish to see;
It follows without understanding
How or where God leads it.
Blind love gives itself forever
To the One it loves
And loses itself in Him.

130. Enter into the Joy of Your Lord

That I suffer—what matters this?
My Lord is in joy, and this gladdens me.
My God and all my good, my heaven, comfort, and blessing—
He who loves You purely thinks little of himself.

131. The Best Offering

Blessed is he who at all times
Can lay before the Lord
A quiet, naked Ground
And a will-less mind.

132. We Look Not at What Is Seen

Draw heart and senses away from what must pass away,
Else you shall never find in God delight, rest, and life.
Live in this world as though you were already dead;
Do it now in love, before you must do it in necessity.

133. How One Is Freed from Sin

If you would be redeemed from sin and made holy,
Sink where you are into God's purity.
Lose yourself in Him with all your sins,
Until you find yourself wholly in God and God in you.

134. Our Heart—God's Sanctuary

I enter into my sanctuary
And remain silent in loving reverence.
In the spirit's quiet darkness,
Far from creatures and the senses,
There dwells God's clarity;
There God is seen in truth.

135. Where God Is Found

God is a quiet Spirit, present everywhere;
Whoever would draw near must not move much.
Let go of images; do not use much effort.
Turn gently into the quiet Spirit—
I know you shall find Him soon.

136. Always in the Present

What has been need not occupy you;
What shall come is not your task.
The moment in which you can give yourself to God
Is too precious—O soul, lose it not!

137. I Live—Yet Not I

My willing, speaking, acting, thinking, understanding
Are full of selfhood; even the best is not pure.
Would that my 'I' were swallowed up as dead in God,
That God might be my life and I His instrument!

138. Trust Not the Serpent

Sin is a crafty thing: it begins as small,
Speaks gently, sweetly, comes in fair disguise;
Later it grows great and dreadful to behold.
Gaze not upon it, O soul—yield it not your will!

139. Life in God

A fish may rise a hundred times with joy in an hour,
Now upward, now down into the depths of water,
Playing gently in the warm sunshine.
So too I live ever in the element of God:
Now sinking into the Ground, now rising in the spirit,
Finding everywhere my resting place—wherever I am.

140. God's Incense Altar

Let your heart be an altar of incense,
From which this one offering rises day and night:
'My God and all my good, my God, You only!
My God, I love You—You shall be mine forever.'

141. He Who Wills God Alone Is Always Still

The worldly soul fears this or that may come,
It worries lest what it loves be taken away;
Now it desires this, now it lacks that,
Now it grieves and frets over what occurs.
I have and will only God—I live content and still,
For evermore my will and my Father's will are one.

142. Softness Brings Greater Pain

Man, do not coddle long your flesh and blood;
Break through at the first hour—take a hero's courage!
What you cannot do, God can. Eternity draws near—
Think on that bitter word: 'O that I had done it!'

143. How Blessed Is a True Christian

How blessed is the one who spends all his time,
Both strength of body and of soul, in God's service;
Who keeps nothing for himself and desires no portion
In eternity but God alone!

144. In the Sanctuary All Is Silent

Let no one ask me how I can be so still.
God is in my Ground; reverence makes me silent.
My heart worships; my spirit beholds Him.
This is my constant work: to bow before my God.

145. No Wind Reaches the Valley

He who enters into reason soon falls into unrest;
He who loves peace must remain in the Ground of simplicity.

146. One Becomes Like Those One Keeps Company With

Worldly company infects—do not make yourself one with it,
Else you shall unawares become a child of the world.
Live instead always in fellowship with God on earth,
So shall you become godly and easily perfected.

147. Jesus to the Soul

If I am to lead you rightly,
You must lose yourself.
Close your eyes;
Do not always wish to see.
Believe—do not understand.
This is the way to rest.

148. Only One of the Two

Seek no pleasure, comfort, nor life in the creature,
And it shall be given you in God, within the Ground of the soul.

149. Happier Than the Angels

> Out of pure love your Savior
> Gave Himself for you unto death;
> Give your whole heart back to Him in love,
> Your dearest life.
> Embrace cross and pain for love's sake—
> No angel can be so happy!

150. A High Estate in Christianity

> Truly, he is a deeply experienced Christian before God
> Who thoroughly believes himself to be a great sinner,
> Who stripped of all trusts in pure grace alone
> And like a beggar looks always to God for every sign.

151. Watch in the Night

> Wait patiently in darkened ways
> And do not turn to creatures,
> O virgin, Bride of God.
> Think not your Bridegroom far away;
> He who remains awake and ready
> Shall see Him at midnight.

152. You Must Be Chaste and Pure

> Remember, Jesus chose you for His bride;
> Let no strange pleasure wound your chaste affection.
> Let your eye be simple, all your thoughts made pure—
> Your Bridegroom looks into your heart.

153. Self-Denial out of Pure Love

To please the Lord alone,
I gladly will deny myself
And every creature too.
Though body and soul should languish,
I count it not, if only
I may be pleasing unto Him.

154. Withdrawn, Content with God

Whatever God gives, takes, or does,
I call it always good.
I yield myself to Him. Lord, only Your will!
In this I remain withdrawn and still.

155. Let the Storm Pass By

When unrest seizes you, be not disturbed;
Stillness itself is how unrest is overcome.
When storms arise, one hides and waits;
When calm returns, the pilgrim goes on.

156. Take Comfort in a Good Evening

Seek no rest in flesh and selfhood
If you have yielded to the guidance of Jesus' Spirit.
One cross follows another—close your eyes;
Out of a thousand deaths comes life eternal.

157. Not on Enemy Ground

World, senses, reason—Satan works within them.
If you enter too deeply, you are in danger.
Remain inwardly gathered, even in your tasks;
In the soul's Ground, in God, no enemy perceives you.

158. Our Chief Occupation

To bow before God as a child,
To incline sweetly into Him—
This alone shall be
Your chief occupation all the day.

159. Guarding the Heart

If you are too scattered among creatures and senses,
Grace and strength will slip away unnoticed.
The new life in you is tender, small, and fragile;
It is easily wounded and must be carefully tended.

160. God Requires Only One Command

Love God with all your heart!
If you fulfill this command,
Man, I tell you plainly:
Then do whatever you will.

161. Adam's Life, Christ's Death

What delights sense and flesh
Brings sorrow to the spirit;
Therefore the cross is dearer to me
Than honor, riches, or delight.

162. Let Yourself Be Led

The wise, the strong, the great
Would lead themselves;
They do not yet know the Shepherd's care.
I, a foolish, weak lamb, must be ruled by Jesus;
I listen for His voice and keep Him in my sight.

163. In Everything, Think Only of God

Let your eye of simplicity be fixed on God
In eating, drinking, walking, standing,
In doing and in refraining, wherever you are.
Let your pure aim in all things be
To please God alone;
Enough, if this aim be attained.

164. Self-Denial and Faith

O soul, you must faithfully deny yourself
And always battle sin and restrain its outbreaks.
Yet let your chief work be this: to grasp Jesus by faith
And allow His Spirit to work within your Ground.
Else—believe me—your heart, despite all outward piety,
Will be a whitewashed tomb full of corruption.

165. How to Do Good Works

To do a good work is needful, useful, and good;
Yet it becomes evil if done by one's own will.
Do all things when, where, and how God wills;
Humble obedience is more than sacrifice.

166. Childlike Estate, Rarely Known

Self-willed, great, and clever—
Such people are found in abundance.
Small, simple, submissive—
Such children are very few.

167. Unformed by Images

Keep the little chamber of your heart
Pure from foreign images.
Let everything remain outside.
God delights in what is bare and empty,
Unburdened and unoccupied—
There He soon makes Himself known.

168. The Precious Adornment

A gentle, quiet childlike spirit,
An unfeigned simplicity of mind—
Such lovely ornament God has chosen;
It leads back to primal innocence.
Whoever allows the Spirit to draw him thus
Already blooms as a lovely flower in paradise
And shall eternally be God's delight.

169. All by Grace

God has much to do with me and with my sin;
Were He not God Himself, He could not rest.
The merits of my works deserve only judgment;
If I am saved at all, it will be by grace.

170. A Child and a Man

He who deeply knows his nothingness
And names God as his all,
Who looks not upon himself
But trusts in God alone,
Who is humbled in himself
Yet raised up in God—
Such a one is both child and man.

171. Leave What Is Trivial; Do What Is Needful

How can a man torment himself
With so much toil over empty things?
The world is not worth a single sigh.
I have a weighty task:
To walk before God and in God as a child,
Thoroughly turned from all else.

172. Complete Surrender

Why stand so long within yourself?
Cast yourself into God and fear not.
Give yourself with full will;
Turn inwardly and forever
From selfhood and from creatures—
So shall God fill you with Himself.

173. Our Homeland Is Near

Soul, close your eyes to the circle of this world;
Sink gently and quietly from self, from place and time.
In the Now of eternity God may be seen;
Your homeland is near—why still run so far?

174. Uprightness Brings Peace and Joy

Ah, better to die a thousand times,
Better to endure all hell's torment,
Than to commit a single sin.
My deepest will does not waver;
My naked Ground stands in God's light—
Such a soul may rejoice.

175. Always the Same Work

Let your only work be to please God
And allow Him to lead you in all things.
Let this be your single task in every action,
And you shall not be scattered among many things.

176. As the Food Is, So Is the Life

Earthly people hunger for the earth;
Their soul's Ground is filled with dark distress.
Ah, hunger only for God—so shall you become divine,
Joyful and luminous, your thirst satisfied.

177. The Heart Must Be Empty and Pure

Remain a stranger to all things
Within the Ground of your soul,
That you may bring God
An empty heart at every hour.
Withdrawn and pure from earthly desires,
So shall you belong to God
And become His friend and child.

178. How Do I Please God?

> Smallness, purity, simplicity—
> These my soul's Friend has chosen.
> Childlike hearts must it be
> With whom He gladly dwells.

179. Food for the Journey

> Self-denial is the food,
> Prayer the daily bread;
> If either is lacking,
> I suffer hunger.

180. He Who Wills One Thing Is Always Still

> Self-will and many desires,
> Though they seem good, bring unrest and pain.
> To depend wholly upon the Lord alone—
> Let this be your work and will, night and day.

181. Jesus to the Soul

> My child, close door and window,
> And return again to rest.
> Into the Ground of your soul
> Let nothing enter that may disturb.
> If you are thus inwardly united with Me,
> I will join Myself to you.

182. What Is Outside Does Not Concern You

What lies outside, let it remain outside;
It brings only unrest.
To walk with God alone in the spirit
Brings rest, joy, and life.

183. Suffering Is Loving

O soul who walks in darkness
And stands inwardly in cross and suffering,
Who wills nothing but God alone—
Your happiness is great: you love the Lord purely.

184. I Await a Visitor

Since I have heard the news
That my Bridegroom wishes to come,
I remain at home day and night,
Lest He come while I am away.

185. To Be Pleasing to God Alone

Whoever seeks to appear something before men
Has already turned away from God.
To look only to God and intend Him alone
Makes you precious in God's sight.

186. Who Can Be Against Us?

Be not troubled when all goes against you;
You must remain bowed and yielded.
The greatest cross gives birth to the greatest blessing;
Nothing can truly oppose the one who loves God.

187. My Creator, My Potter

Through outward adversity,
Through inward cross and suffering,
You are made humble and pure.
Like clay, let yourself be shaped
In the hands of your Creator—
He fashions you with care.

188. Be Still in Cross and Pain

Remain yielded to God, joyful and still
In dryness, cross, and darkness.
Let God and His will be enough for you—
So shall you stand firm into eternity.

189. Stillness Is Your Praise in Zion

In God's presence, be still—
Your mouth, your thoughts, your desires, your will.
The highest Majesty is worthy
To be honored with silence.

190. Love Makes All Things Light

He who knows God's faithfulness and love
Knows no toil anymore.
Self-denial he calls delight,
The shame of the cross his honor.

191. It Is Revealed to the Childlike

> Self-seeking inquiry cannot grasp
> God's truth, work, and light.
> Only a small and pure child
> Finds God's wonders while at rest.

192. Attentiveness to God

> A gentle, loving attentiveness
> To God in the Ground of your soul—
> This single, small, pure work
> Will easily unite you with God.

193. The Forbidden Tree

> The brief pleasure of sin, the vanity of the world,
> Is a forbidden tree—be not deceived.
> Whoever keeps his delight turned inward toward God
> Will triumph with Christ over world and foe.

194. Cease from Your Own Doing

> It pains me to see so many good souls
> Tormenting themselves with much activity
> Yet bearing no fruit or progress.
> Love God and remain near Him; cease your own working,
> And yield yourself wholly to Him if you would be sanctified.

195. The Yielded One Is Rich

Now you desire this, now that,
And are never content.
He has the Giver with the gifts
Who is wholly yielded unto God.

196. Self-Denial and Prayer

Self-denial and prayer are sisters who love one another.
Whoever casts one away has driven both away.
Whoever seeks one must take the other also;
Whoever loves and practices both will soon be sanctified.

197. God the Lord; I the Servant

God wills to rule me as King
And guide me as Shepherd.
His will and sign alone shall stand.
My Lord, command—I will bow.
Lead as You will; I will be silent.
You are Creator; I am creature.

198. Serenity of Spirit

As the air appears on pleasant days—
Clear, bright, and still—
So let your spirit be.
Then you shall see God within
And be pleasing unto Him;
His wondrous light will fill your soul.

199. He Who Can Taste God

God tastes good and sweet—only empty your mouth.
Whoever would taste Him truly must taste nothing else.

200. Holy Endurance

God wills to be the One who works within you;
You must endure His working.
Remain inwardly small, still, and close to Him
At all times.

201. Cause of Unsteadiness

Ask not why you are unsteady:
You do not remain within with God.
Ask not why a little child falls
When it does not cling to its mother.

202. Give Much, and You Shall Have Much

If you continually return to God
What He bestows on you,
You shall receive still more
And can live content.

203. Loving in Suffering

In suffering think: God remains God,
Whether I be glad or sorrowful;
Therefore in cross and need
He must be loved as truly as in comfort.

204. How to Obtain What You Desire

Deny your longing and your pleasures,
And soon you shall receive what you desire.
If your delight is in God alone,
You are free from unrest, pain, and burden.

205. Stillness Is Not Idleness

When God makes you still, fear not
And call it not idleness
To yield yourself to His drawing.
Should not the creature keep still
When the Creator wills to work,
And embrace its God?

206. Praise Brings Harm

A good work done in secret
Out of pure love, to please God only,
Brings great gain;
But what all men praise
Has mostly already taken its reward.

207. United to One Alone

Remain a stranger to creatures, and you shall be united
    with God;
Two masters cannot be served at once.

208. All for the Lord Alone

In all your doing look to God alone,
And do not ask whether others will approve;
Else you turn outward, and your work is not pure.
In the Ground of simplicity remain inwardly in all things.

209. How One May Become Rich

Who would be rich and blessed,
Let him keep his spirit always poor and empty
Of the desire and love of all things.
Sink into your deep nothingness;
Let God alone be your salvation and your good—
This will bring heaven into you.

210. Holy Foolishness

Live without will, desire, and care,
Hidden in your Ground, in God.
I know that such a 'foolish' child
Finds the best treasure without running about.

211. Denial Brings Contentment

He who seeks to satisfy
His desires and his own will in everything
Lives always discontent.
But he who gives himself to self-denial,
Unmoved in love and suffering,
Has conquered the world and himself.

212. The Fairest Love

How pure, how fair is that love
Which honors the Beloved in the cross without comfort,
Which intends God alone and does not look at itself,
Which still loves on, though body and soul be spent.

213. Weak Love and Strong Love

Weak love complains when it does not see the friend;
It is easily discouraged and withdraws from suffering.
Strong love forgets itself and its own repose;
If the Beloved is well, it too is satisfied.

214. If You Love Me, Suffer with Me

O soul, you who are troubled
In days of cross and suffering,
Show now that you love truly;
Love cannot complain.
Look not on yourself and your pain;
Enter into your Lord's joy.

215. Courage Wins the Fight

He who would follow God must be bold and brave,
Not always living in fear, anxiety, and complaint.
Yield yourself with courage and count no pain too great;
Faith will give you light, and love will give you strength.

216. The Nature of Divine Love

It must be true love—
Steadfast, inward, free, and pure.
It is the soul's food and life,
Hell's poison, sin's death;
It strengthens and comforts in every need.
Empty out your heart—God can give it.

217. The Leading of Divine Love

Love is sweet, yet also strict;
Its leading often passes through narrow ways.
It leaves no room for selfhood;
Its sharp eye tests heart and inmost parts.
Only yield yourself wholly to its leading—
And what is narrow will at last grow wide.

218. Indifferent in All Things

Wherever you are, and however it goes with you—
Now humbled, now lifted up;
Now in joy, now in pain;
Now despised, now honored—
Remain indifferent, undisturbed,
Only inwardly united with God.

219. Care for Only One Thing

Be free of all anxious care; only care for this above all:
How you may please God best at all times.

220. Fear Only One Thing

A Christian fears nothing—neither need, nor death, nor pain;
He fears only that he might displease God.

221. Fire and Pain Make Pure

To stand in darkness, seeing only sin with grief,
Stripped of comfort and strength, of grace (as one supposes),
And through one's own fault robbed of every virtue—
O highest trial of suffering for God-minded hearts!
Thus fire melts away the deepest selfhood;
Thus a vale of sorrow leads to true holiness.

222. The Dreadfulness of Selfhood

The more I sink, the more God is exalted;
The smaller I become in myself, the more He is honored
   in me.
He who forgets himself, who loses, stands best in God;
The slightest selfhood is worthy of hell.

223. The Greatest Loves the Least

The most exalted Being of God
Has chosen only childlike hearts
To be His throne and His delight.
To the great and clever He remains far;
In the Ground of simplicity He gladly dwells
And makes Himself wholly common to such.

224. The Happiest Solitude

To be alone with God alone
Is the happiest life;
But whoever would be united with Him
Must bid farewell to all.

225. He Who Runs Out Often Neglects His House

One does not remain inward enough;
Therefore one is weak and miserable.
He who lies always at Jesus' breasts
Becomes holy, joyful, and content.

226. Let Yourself Not Desire

What you look upon with desire
Imprints itself within you.
Look upon none but Jesus—
And blessed shall you be.

227. He Who Stays at Home Shares Out the Spoil

By running and striving
One does not win the treasure.
He who can remain at home
In the still Ground—he has it.

228. To Turn Inward Is to Do Penance

Whoever has sinned,
Let him after the deed
Turn inward with grief,

Thoroughly away from sin,
Gently as a child,
Only into Jesus' heart.

229. The Holy Dead

So long as anything lives in you, you remain in distress;
He who would live blessed must die to all.

230. What You Seek Is What You Find

Lose yourself utterly; let the creature vanish.
You still seek yourself—therefore you cannot find God.

231. O Blessed Hours—Now I Have Found It!

I can sigh no more—I have what I desire;
What I sought far off, I now find near within me.
My constant prayer is that I be silent still,
Behold my treasure, and embrace Him with content.

232. Will-lessness

How blessed, when one's own will
Lies in God like a dead thing—still—
And when an inward, gentle inclination
May be bent this way and that by God.

233. Pure Intention toward God

He who intends and loves himself
Is disturbed, ever sorrowful,
Pressed down by many things.

Let your eye of simplicity in all things
Intend nothing but God and His good pleasure—
So shall you remain quiet, glad, and free.

234. To Serve God Is to Be Blessed

To please God alone,
To renounce one's dearest pleasure,
To offer Him always
One's heart and will,
And to live with Him in familiar communion—
Consider what blessedness!

235. Make Room in Your Heart for God Alone

Creatures, depart from my heart;
Leave this place wholly to the Creator alone.
My all I lay at His feet;
He is my treasure—and I am wholly His.

236. What Is God's Will?

If you ask what God's will is,
Look not around at many things.
It is one in all.
Keep your Ground still in God.
He who wills nothing from himself
Can please God very easily.

237. Jesus to the Soul

My child, go not too far from home;
Pour yourself out never completely.
Even in your work remain steady.

Hold My hand like a child;
Let your eyes be turned inward always
To your Friend within.

238. Remain Turned Inward

Let all go—return into your Ground.
The enemy often lures outward under fair appearance.
He who turns into the sensible world without need
Is weakened and disturbed without noticing.

239. The Fairest Heart

How fair is that heart which, emptied of all,
Holds nothing within but God's good pleasure—
Which, through much cross and suffering, melted and cleansed,
Bears the highest Majesty in the still Ground.

240. The Most Tender Guest

God loves to dwell in plain little children,
Yet the smallest thing can hinder this tender Guest:
A little self-will, a secret desire disturbs.
How pure must that one be who longs for such a Guest!

241. Death Leads Me Out of Distress

When I think of the state where one sins no more,
Where no selfhood can disturb rest in God,
Where one loves God purely and gives Him perfect honor—
Then I desire death, that I might return into that place.

242. The Nearest Way to Heaven

Do what you do not will, and leave what you do will—
This is the nearest road to blessedness.

243. Free from Everything

To everything you have, cling so lightly
That in a moment you can calmly give it up.
Whatever God Himself is not, let it all be the same to you;
Believe it: such a 'poor' man possesses a kingdom of heaven.

244. Everything in Its Order

A will that yields, gentle and pliant as a child;
A mind free from foreign images, full of still loving thought;
A heart loosed from all, loving the Godhead purely;
Reason and senses—blind and dead: blessed is he who can be so.

245. What Holds Me Back?

You complain it is hard; you ask, 'What holds me back?'
Reason and self-will hinder your course.
Think not too much—believe blindly without seeing,
And remain will-less; so shall you walk more easily.

246. Familiarity with God

Hold God as your Friend, near you in your Ground;
As your Bridegroom, to whom you are bound.
Be familiar with Him; let Him be your joy;
Remain inwardly with Him in the Now of eternity.

247. Know Yourself

How can a man still complain of others?
I lack patience even to bear myself!
He who knows himself deeply and feels himself rightly
Will gladly be the servant of the greatest sinner.

248. Humility Is Good against Falling

Be small and turned inward; live neither proud nor secure.
In poverty, where you are, cling to God in your Ground.
Nothing is yours, you weak creature;
Only a slender thread of grace holds you.

249. I Already Have My Good Within Me

O what blessedness, to carry one's good always with oneself
And one's best Friend in the Ground of the soul!
One no longer wanders about asking creatures,
When the Creator Himself makes Himself known to the spirit.

250. Freedom of the Children of God

O noble freedom—when the will, withdrawn
From all that is not God, stands inwardly will-less;
Free from anxiety and striving, living lifted up in peace,
Where nothing touches or disturbs it in the Father's bosom.

251. The Carefree Life

How still and safely one can live
When one has wholly yielded oneself to God
And no longer thinks and worries for oneself!

To keep yourself in the present
And let Providence rule
Makes you lighter and carries you forward.

252. Let Your Light Shine

He who, stripped within himself, looks to God alone
Can shine as a light of virtue to God's honor;
He who beholds his own virtue is not the most devout—
Out of our nothingness God can gain the best praise.

253. Through Hell to Heaven

The fairest building of true holiness
Is founded by the Lord in misery, cross, and death;
One feels condemnation first, then blessedness—
He who loses his soul finds it again in God.

254. Hold Back Nothing

He who loves or wills something that is not God Himself
Lengthens his misery and hinders his peace.
Purely down to the Ground—upright, without deceit!
He who would be united with God must become
    withdrawn.

255. Break the Will, Not the Head

Head-breaking will never find
The Lord's presence and teaching;
Ah, break only your will!
Keep your heart emptied and pure—
Simple, inward, glad, and small—
Soon will God fill you.

256. Prayer and Solitude

Right prayer I call the soul's bread;
Solitude my bed that refreshes me.
If I neglect either without need,
I grow weary and easily entangled in sleep.

257. Jesus to the Soul

Ah, remain turned inward and always on watch;
You foolish child do not know your own harm.
Your wandering out, alas, neglects many graces
Which My motherly heart has so richly intended for you!

258. The Preciousness of the Time of Grace

A moment of this short time of grace
Is more precious than all the goods of the earth.
Lose it not—the eternity is coming;
Here one sows; there one shall reap.

259. God's Dwelling

The center of your being
God has chosen as His dwelling.
Turn gently in—there His Godhead
Reveals its presence.

260. Divine Jealousy

Remain pure, detached, and always watchful;
Your Soul-Bridegroom is exceedingly jealous.
He allows His bride no life, comfort, or rest,
Because He alone will be it—all in one thing.

261. Blessed Are the Poor

O great blessedness—to be stripped of all
And have on earth nothing more than God alone!

262. Love Must Be Heartfelt, Yet Pure

The brethren must be loved with the heart—
But love them purely, in God alone;
Else it only hinders and brings sorrow.
What is divine makes one united with God.

263. Among Saints One Becomes Holy

To keep friendship with God's friends
Brings grace, strength, and a thousand blessings.
He who stands inwardly united with God
Draws other souls in with him.

264. The Mirror of the Godhead

Your pure Ground of the soul is the Godhead's mirror;
The slightest selfhood dims its shine.
Touch nothing unclean! Where you are truly still,
In God's light you shall soon behold God Himself within you.

265. The Bridegroom and the Bride

My Bridegroom's eye beholds
Me always as His bride,
And shows me where the blemishes lie.
He, my Friend, is Himself so fair;
Therefore He would also gladly see me
Without wrinkle, without spot.

266. Keep Your Gaze Fixed on God

So long as I look upon my Friend alone,
I stand secure, unwavering, deep in peace—
O pure eye of simplicity, innocent attention!
But as soon as I turn toward myself and creatures,
I become timid and weak and disturb myself in all things;
And whatever I do becomes a stained work.

267. Full Surrender to God

'My choosing is done; my willing sinks away;
However You arrange it, my Lord, I am well content,'
So speaks the Ground of my soul, though reason still complains:
'Lord, let only Your will be done; You need not ask me.'

268. Life out of Death

The deeper you give yourself into dying,
The higher shall you be led into true life.
Out of darkness comes light, out of cross and suffering joy—
He has not the one, who still shrinks from the other.

269. In Inward Purifications

One sees the dross when it separates from the gold.
He who would have virtue must first endure vice;
If only your will is free and evil is a burden to you,
However ugly you seem to yourself—you truly have virtue.

270. Medicine against Curiosity

Man's eye soon seeks and loves now this, now that:
Now something new is here, now something fair is there.
He plays with toys because he has nothing better.
Ah poor man—had you found God Himself within you,
I know this fairest good would hold heart and mind bound;
Your curiosity would be stilled, your lusting eye satisfied.

271. Looking Ahead Makes Safe Walking

What God has done from eternity and into the eternities
I will not dispute much.
In the present I keep watch;
I am only a child in the house—I let the Father act.
To love Him is my work, and He does His own matters;
In the end I shall see that He has done it well.

272. Fire and Oil

A dark, tormenting fire is your soul within itself;
Let your Savior be within you your soothing balm of oil.
Sink out of selfhood; let God thoroughly possess you;
Then shall you become bright and glad—then the soul triumphs.

273. High Light Is Not Yet the Substance

Many have light about high states
And still long lack the true substance.
Light is a flower that can easily blow away—
See what fruit remains in you after cold and storm.

274. Where the Ark Comes, Dagon Must Fall

Forget sin and cling inwardly to God;
Leave Him your heart bare, that He may live there as Lord.
When His presence appears in your Ground,
Darkness and sin must vanish at once.

275. Seeking and Finding Are Two Things

Bind yourself not too tightly to forms and ways;
One does not always seek God—one must also find Him.
He who is still seeking runs and works much;
He who has found Him enjoys and is still.

276. If You Desire Comfort, Remain Turned Inward

To remain turned inward in God and live in communion
Will give your spirit light, joy, and heaven.
Sink out of selfhood; turn away from the creature—
It brings you only darkness, pain, and hell.

277. To Look at Yourself Helps Little

Think not much about yourself; let God be your aim.
He who is always watching himself is not thereby freed from
   himself.

278. The Most Useful Man

He who wills nothing and does nothing
Except that he rests in God, yielded,
Even if he would not appear to be anything—

Truly does more to God's honor
And to his neighbor's good
Than others who 'mean well.'

279. Help Comes by Turning Inward and Stillness

With so many good souls, I know,
God would unite Himself in marriage
If they would only hold still for Him—
Turned inward and as God wills.
Ah, in stillness one grows weary;
If comfort and peace do not soon come,
If only night and dryness come,
One turns outward again to the creature.

280. God Gives Alms

God gives gifts: he who is rich shall have nothing;
A poor beggar receives God and His gifts.

281. The Pilgrim Mind

My body and the world are to me a strange house;
I think: Let it go—you will soon depart.
He who lives here as a citizen undertakes great things;
He calls me poor and foolish—and yet he himself is a fool.

282. Turned Inward and Undisturbed

Remain always turned inward in the gentle Ground of peace!
Nothing weakens the spirit more than to be disturbed.
As soon as you are moved, sit down in stillness
And return, as soon as you can, to your rest again.

283. Desire Good without Disturbance

One may indeed desire what is good,
But one must not be disturbed about it
If it does not come as one wills.
Self-love drives violently;
Pure love remains gentle
And keeps the Ground still in everything.

284. The Forgotten Citizen

Blessed is he for whom this world is like a foreign land,
Who lives small and quiet, despised and unknown,
Who seeks favor, comfort, and praise from God alone,
Who, stranger to all and dead to it, lives turned inward
    in God.

285. Withdrawal

He who desires much
Is much disturbed;
He who wills nothing
Remains always still.
In comfort and joys,
In fear and sufferings,
Remain withdrawn
In God's peace.

286. God Alone Must Be Master

Do never what you will; rather lie down in stillness,
That God alone may will and work in you according to His
    mind.

287. Making Necessity into Virtue

Need presses me indeed to live always turned inward;
I myself am poor and weak, and the world gives only pain.
All my salvation stands in clinging to God in the spirit;
Thus grace upon grace flows out of Him into me.

288. Compassionate Love

With simplicity, love, and compassion
Look upon your neighbor's misery.
Think no evil; for God can well help the poor
And can also help you remain yielded.

289. Keep Jesus Company

Where run you—to vain things?
How can you bear it in your heart
That you leave your Friend alone?
He so gladly would be with you—
Should you not also look upon Him?
He is near you—only turn inward.

290. God Visits the Solitary

Remain a stranger to all things. If you are alone within yourself,
God will soon visit you and make Himself common to you.

291. To Please Only One

He who would please all men
Is turned outward and never still
And cannot please God.

I am only my God's servant:
If I can do it rightly for Him,
Let men complain.

292. Let God Care for It

Be still and yield yourself to God in all your affairs;
Be anxious for nothing—your Father will do it well.
Care only for God alone;
He will be your guardian.

293. Divine Wilderness

O quiet wilderness,
Free from world and senses—
To live with God in the Ground,
Where nothing enters
But God and I alone,
To whom I wholly yield myself!

294. To Serve God Is to Be Free

To be one's own lord and master,
To live after one's own mind and will,
Does not make you free—it brings only anxiety and pain;
Thus the noble spirit floats as in a prison.
He who would truly be free here on earth
Must become the slave of my God.

295. As God Wills You, So Be Still

He who is inward need not force his spirit,
Nor by violence press into a certain state.
Light or night, refreshment or pain—
As God sets you, so must you be willing to be.

296. My Secret Is with Me

Your joys and your sufferings—
Tell and lament not to everyone.
Be content in both
When the Lord looks upon you.

297. Union of the Will

My will leaves world, reason, and senses behind
And unites gently with God in the still Ground.
In the heart, not in the head, God reveals Himself.
Become only a still child—and you shall find Him at once.

298. The Fair and Easy Art

Only gently and still look upon God,
Think no more of world and self;
Walk with Him as with your Friend—
O fair art, O easy teaching!

299. He Who Loves, Finds

Men seek God, they work, they run about;
Ah, only love—leave what scatters you.
A still spirit is God's sanctuary;
There He will reveal Himself to simplicity.

300. The One Main Business

To turn out of time with heart, mind, and thought
And sink inwardly into eternity—
Let this be your main business from morning to night.
Practice this unto death—and you have accomplished all.

301. The Easy Way to Holiness

The short and easy way to true holiness
Is this: to forget all things—and even yourself;
To think on God with heartfelt inwardness,
And, childlike, sink into His boundless Being.

302. He Who Has Nothing Has God

Though comfort and light may fail you,
Yet God is not therefore lacking.
Be still within, and hold your nothingness
In place of comfort and of light.
Soul, believe it: he who truly has nothing at all
Has God—and in Him, everything indeed.

303. Whoever Denies God

God alone is enough; whoever desires something more
Denies and dishonors the all-satisfying Good.

304. The Son Makes Truly Free

Would you be truly freed
From yourself and all things?
Make yourself only one with Christ,
And it will become altogether easy for you.

305. Having as Not Having

If loss and damage of things still grieve you,
You have not possessed and loved them in God.

306. Who Is a Saint?

Place not the ground of holiness in this or that;
Deny yourself wholly, and let God have you thoroughly.
He who purely intends God alone in all his doing—
He is a saint, and free from every pain.

307. Not All That Glitters Is Gold

Not all is good that outwardly seems so;
Not all is evil that men call so.
The work is good and great where God is meant within it—
Else your doing is small, and there is not much good in it.

308. Die While You Live

Die—die while you live; never say, 'It is enough!'
He who thinks he has finished is already caught in deception.

309. The Noble Ground of the Soul

I dwell most gladly in the noble Ground of the soul,
Withdrawn from creature, reason, and the senses,
Where the Godhead makes itself known to my spirit;
Here I live free and glad in deep, hidden peace.

310. God Alone Must Be Your Aim

Soul, look only upon God—not upon what you do or are;
He who is always watching himself is always in unrest.

311. The Safest Retreat

My Jesus bears the curse that else had fallen on me
And by His death opens the Father's heart to me.
Flee, little turtledove—flee into these clefts,
Out of every creature, if you would be safe!

312. What True Prayer Is

To pray aright is to cleave to God in the Ground with love,
And to yield one's whole will into God's will.
In suffering one often 'prays' and yet does not truly mean it;
And many a one does not pray who seems to pray much.

313. Seek It in the Right Place

Men seek something they do not even know;
Therefore they seek amiss and never find it.
You seek rest and joy—who would not grant it you?
Ah, turn wholly to God: He is what you lack.

314. Knowing and Doing

Most men would now
Know much, but do little;
He who would rightly serve God
Must do much and know little.

315. Waste Not the Time

The time of grace is short; the work is great and weighty.
Soul, do not hold yourself up with things that are nothing.
To deny yourself is your work—and to love your God.
Blessed is he who spends his time upon this work!

316. Holy War-Craft

God ever wages war
With sin and selfhood;
If you in your soul
Now choose God's side,
Then the enemy stands alone—
And soon there will be peace.

317. You Shall Not Steal

Man, love your God alone—
Else are you truly already a thief,
For you rob God of what is His.
Your heart belongs to God alone;
Seek joy in Him, seek rest in Him—
Consider it well, if you believe it!

318. Whoever Yields to God, God Holds Fast

In suffering, cross, and need you must yield yourself to God;
Let Him always act, and remain without self-will.
We make our own pain by our resistance.
Give your soul only up—then it falls into God's lap.

319. Adam's Death Is Christ's Life

The more the life of nature in you is brought to die,
The more you shall behold Christ's life within your soul.
Therefore slay what you can; shun neither cross nor suffering:
Whatever you lose of the old, you find new in Christ.

320. My All Must Be Jesus Alone

Only Jesus is my salvation, in whom I stand;
Only Jesus is the spring from which grace and truth flow;
Only Jesus is the image on which alone I must look;
Only Jesus is the Shepherd who ever leads and feeds me;
Only Jesus is the power by which I overcome;
Only Jesus is the Ground of true holiness;
Only Jesus is my treasure, in whom I find all;
Only Jesus shall it be in time and in eternity.

321. The Most Blessed Bondage

O sweet bondage—to be caught in love,
Where Jesus' gentle nod is the bond of our will
And all love is turned wholly toward Him!
I know such a one will not desire to be 'free.'

322. The Blessed Hermit

Let the whole world—its fairest and its sweetest—
Be to your spirit like a foreign wilderness.
Let your heart be a secret little hut;
There retire continually into God.

323. God Must Be Sought in Spirit

God is Spirit; therefore whoever would find Him
Must live in the spirit, not in the senses.
Leave all things and only hold yourself still to Him;
So is He near, and will soon give Himself to you.

324. The Best School of Virtue

The best school of virtue is your own soul-Ground;
When all is silent within you and you sink into it,
Wisdom teaches you with her own mouth
And will essentially bestow all virtues upon you.

325. The Greatest Monarch

He who is dead to selfhood
And lives only unto God at all times
Is the greatest king on earth.
He has and does always what he wills,
And in all storms remains still—
Who would not die, to become so?

326. Where God Appears, the Other Gives Way

As soon as one has found within himself the Highest Good,
Money and goods and all cares fall away.
A better aim holds love wholly bound;
Thus one lives rich and satisfied in simple, blind faith.

327. Lord, If I Have Only You...

Men may give or take,
May honor or shame me,
May love me—or not;
Whether it be dark or light,
Whether I be sorrowful or glad,
In pleasantness or in suffering—
If I have only God, I am still,
And have what I would have.

328. Through Narrowness to Splendor

Faint not, O soul, in paths of cross and suffering!
When gold is in the fire, the refiner is near.
The Lord scours His dearest children the most;
The way to the kingdom goes by Golgotha.

329. Everything Has Its Time

To deny, to believe, to strive, to suffer—
This is our work in this time;
To enjoy, to see, to rest in joy
Will follow in eternity.

330. He Who Goes Out of Self Stands in Freedom

How blessed is the man who has gone out of himself—
Stripped in spirit, living only by faith—
Who wills nothing but to cling to God for comfort,
Who like an eagle freely soars above all things!
Then the spirit gains room; the heart becomes free and light.
Let him thank God in humility who has reached this state!

331. Will-less, Free from Care

You must, O soul, only hold yourself before God
Inward, will-less, and without care, in stillness.
Sink like a child into your Father's lap
And let Him rule with you and over all.

332. The Divine Idleness

O divinely fair 'idleness'—
To stop one's own working
And let God only act;
Where one speaks nothing, wills nothing, does nothing,
And rests inwardly only in the Lord!
Reason cannot grasp this.

333. The Miser

Creatures, be gone—I can well do without you,
Since the Creator Himself makes Himself one with my spirit.
He who possesses the Highest Good can desire nothing more;
He whom God does not satisfy must surely be a miser.

334. Sinking into God

How blessed is he who in faith
Loses body and soul into God's sea,
Who gently sinks beneath time, place, and creature
In the Ground of the soul, where no storm touches him.

335. Shut It Out—And You Have Rest

Remain a stranger to the creature and withdrawn;
If you let it in, it disturbs your peace.
God alone is enough; God alone brings rest—
Hold yourself only inwardly; shut the doors.

336. How One Becomes Taught of God

Much searching of reason does not reach God's light;
So long as you do sin, you know not the truth.
Only make your heart empty, gentle, and yielded to God;
Thus can you easily grasp God and His truth.

337. Whoever Knows God Must Love Him

Come, children of men—taste and see
How sweet God is, how gentle His yoke.
Turn inward, and you shall see it.
He who has essentially found within himself
This treasure—God Himself—
Will never again go outward from Him.

338. Who Is the Greatest Sinner

See you the righteous, see you the sinner—
Think at once, in sincerity:
I am worse, weaker, lesser,
And lay yourself beneath all.

339. The Joyful Cloister-Life

My soul-Ground is my sweet cell
Wherein I live united with my God;
There springs for me the rich fountain of life—
Ah, that I might always remain shut in there!

340. Eternity Is Not So Far

Still eternity is near to our spirit
When God has loosed it from time and creature.
Turn out of the many into the One—God is only One.
O blessed he who has found this good in his Ground!

341. Let Me Rest—I Have Work to Do

What is it to me what the world and other men do,
Since in the Ground with God I can rest in hiddenness?
My new and old work is this: that I, in spirit, continually
Keep company with the Highest Majesty—God Himself.

342. Yielded to God Alone

I have yielded myself to God;
I will also live only to Him
And love Him everywhere.
I am in His hands;
He may lead and turn me—
If only I please Him.

343. How One Should Suffer Well

Would you bear a cross according to God's will,
Bear it gently and secretly, without complaining.
Look only upon God and not upon your pain;
What He gives you cannot be evil.

344. He Who Follows and Trusts Sees Wonders

Would you behold God's wonders?
Follow, in faith, His drawing;
Learn childlike trust in Him—
Let Him alone be enough for you.

345. Death Brings the True Life

Continually dying to nature,
Giving one's lust and will
To God in love;
Dead to all and a stranger to it,
Only in spirit one with God—
This brings the true life.

346. He Who Loves God Only Remains Undisturbed

Would you be ever glad?
Rejoice only in God alone.
Comfort and joy in other things
Must at last bring sorrow.

347. An Angelic Spectacle

How fair and lovely it is to see
When the righteous spirit, content in God,
Lies so gently and still in pain and suffering
And kisses his Father's good hand
That, in love, has sent him the cross!

348. God in the Heart Comforts in Pain

Ah souls—hasten! die gladly to nature
And to all selfhood, that you may find God within.
In need and death nothing avails but God in the heart;
This holds in the fire the trial, when show and delusion
    vanish.

349. Bitter in the Mouth—Yet Healthful

When God shows Himself near to the spirit,
Then the heaviest suffering becomes light;
Yet it often brings no less fruit and blessing
If in darkness too one can lie still in God.

350. God Loves Those Who Love Him

Ask not whether God loves you—only seek to please Him.
Deny sin and the world, and also yourself above all.
The conclusion does not deceive: if you love God in deed,
Be assured that He has loved you.

351. Always Ready

Perhaps this very hour may be my last;
Therefore must I carry my soul in my hands,
That when Jesus comes I may freely and calmly say:
There, Jesus—my spirit lays itself into Your hand.

352. Rule of Life

Not learned and not honored,
Unknown and turned inward;
Having nothing more, caring nothing more;
Will-less, hidden in God,
Belonging only to eternity—
This shall be my rule.

353. The Best Land Is Unknown

He who can truly die to himself
Will inherit the land of peace
That blooms in the Ground of the soul,
Where place and time vanish,
Where spirit is joined with Spirit,
Where one sees light and life.

354. Remain at Rest—God Speaks to You

Your soul-friend, O soul, is not far;
He is within you. Only remain withdrawn
And inwardly still—then He gladly speaks to you.
His speaking anoints the Ground with deep peace.

355. Yielded in Faith

Reasonings of reason—be silent!
I follow the Lord freely, without seeing.
Blind faith shows the track
How one must go unto the death of selfhood.

356. Walking in Truth

He who lives in the light of truth,
Loves God inwardly and exalts Him,
And continually despises himself,
Bows beneath all men,
Willingly receives cross and suffering,
Because he beholds his nothingness.

357. Withdrawal Gladdens Only the Spirit

True withdrawal

Brings our spirit peace and joy—
A pure, gentle, free life.
The flesh gains nothing on this path;
Selfhood is not concerned with it;
Therefore give it nothing at all.

358. The Shepherd's Voice

When I am unawares scattered into the senses,
A gentle drawing soon calls me back from within.
So faithfully my Shepherd cares and guards His little sheep—
If only I could remain gathered in Him, unwavering!

359. Jesus to the Soul

My child, give Me your heart, your understanding, and your will;
Henceforth let only My nod guide your doing and leaving undone.
Look always only unto Me, and keep yourself still and small,
That you may will, love, and think only in Me.

360. To a Troubled Soul

Let fall what torments you;
Tell Jesus what you lack.
Your Helper is not far;
He helps so willingly.
Only yield yourself to His hand
And give Him heart and will;
Let His drawing quiet you—
So shall every bond be broken.

361. Bare and Pure Must You Be

Ah, were my spirit so pure, so imageless and still—
Like a white sheet on which one would write—
Soon would the Son of God, by the beams of His light,
Paint His wondrous image in my Ground.

362. The Rest of the Spirit

If the discomforts of the flesh can still disturb the spirit's rest,
Then the rest is not yet deep, not pure, not firm.
The spirit can return more freely to its rest
The more tightly one keeps the flesh bound to the cross.

363. Remain Very Near to the Shepherd

Inwardly, inwardly must you hold yourself
Near to Jesus—
Look upon Him continually
And let Him rule.
Light and life, strength and grace—
One has them only in Jesus.

364. Mighty in the Weak

When you feel keenly your deep inability,
Sink in humility into your nothingness.
Let your stripped spirit lie deep in Jesus—
In your weakness the Highest would be mighty.

365. The Lord Is My Strength

If I do not remain always turned inward in Jesus,
I am unawares disturbed by the least thing.
In Jesus I am strong—when senses and thoughts
Stand in His love, I go without wavering.

366. If You Love Me, Lose Yourself

He who loves his soul preserves it diligently;
And he who loves God purely must lose his soul.
How blessed it is, thus lost—
No enemy may ever touch it in God's hand.

367. Above the Clouds No Wind Blows

How blessed is a heart that lives withdrawn,
And rises above joy and sorrow, only into God!
It stands firm and still even in changes,
For through death it has entered into life.

368. Were I Freed from Selfhood!

This dreadful 'own' brings the spirit so much burden.
Ah, could I wholly sink from myself and become nothing
With Christ in death—so that, in pure innocence,
I might live only out of God, in God, before God!

369. Chosen—Wedded to God

Consider: God, the Highest Being,
Has chosen you for His delight
And bought you for His bride.
Pure—alone you are His;
Love Him only, intend Him purely;
His eye is ever upon you.

370. The Work of Love

Love is so pure and tender
When it reveals itself in us;
It permits nothing 'own' to be seen.
The whole heart must be God's;
What God is not, it lets not in;
The spirit must stand withdrawn.

371. Time and Eternity

A moment of still eternity,
Which one even here may taste in spirit,
Is more precious—so I say it without fear—
Than a time of a hundred thousand years.

372. How One Bears the Cross Aright

Can you live with the cross
Only in Him who gave the cross—
Withdrawn, gentle, and still—
Soon the burden of the cross vanishes,
Because one finds God in the cross,
And so the Father wills it.

373. God Alone Must Be Your Aim

Selfhood always seeks something for itself;
It asks for God, yet means only His gifts.
He who intends God purely in all things
Can have God always—even in dryness.

374. How God Is Found

O soul, sink from your own will;
Turn inward and let yourself be stilled.
In the Ground of the soul God is near us;
He who loses all finds Him there.

375. The Blessed Free Spirit

A free spirit, raised in God, stands
Bound by nothing but God's love alone.
Nothing moves it, for lifted in spirit
It leaves beneath itself world, senses, and nature.

376. Always Still and Clear

Hold yourself inward, still, and pure
Like a clear little stream,
That the Highest's love-sun
May shine into you with light and delight!

377. Be Loose and Free from All

Let go what you have
Held fast with love—
It keeps you bound as well.
He who can turn to God
Heartily, freely, and purely
Soon finds the treasure.

378. It Remains a Gentle Yoke

It is not hard—ah no—
To be a true Christian,
To stand denied in all things.
Ah, only remain turned inward
And make yourself known to God—
So it becomes easier.

379. Yet a Little While

Soon my last little hour is here
When I shall go to the Lord;
Then I shall be near Him forever
And see Him clearly in the light.
Meanwhile I bear, a little longer,
With Jesus here, His yoke of the cross.

380. Jesus to the Soul

O soul, I dwell and rest so gladly in you—
Ah, do also dwell unwaveringly in Me!
My loving heart stands open to you;
Can you hope for anything better?

381. What Love Does Is All Good

He who lives in love—his work is pure and good:
He eats, drinks, sleeps, and whatever else he does.

382. The Best Gifts

I do not await visions,
Gifts of wonders, lofty lights;
To have the cross and pure love—
I value more than all gifts.

383. Jesus to the Soul

My precious child—ah, love Me,
For I so dearly love you
That I would give Myself wholly to you.
How can you think of anything else?

384. In All Doing, Rest in One

I do this and that; I go here and there—
My spirit stands unmoved in its point of rest.
In the Ground it beholds the Lord's face
And takes not to heart what may happen outwardly.

385. God Is Here—Look, Within You

God is nearer to you than you are to yourself.
Would you draw near to Him, you must not move much.
Leave what is sensory; remain will-less and still;
Turn your attention inward—there God would show
    Himself.

386. Self-Will Disturbs Stillness

The most hidden self-will
Stains your work and disturbs stillness;
Then it becomes night in the soul.
As you can move your hand,
So must your will also lie
Without its own choosing—in God's power.

387. The Best Teacher

He who remains still and inward, turned into the soul-
    Ground,
Is guided and taught by God in secret—
How he should let go of all things, even of himself,
And grasp God, the one Good, in pure love.

388. The Most Blessed Homeland

The Godhead's pure, still Being
I have chosen for my dwelling.
There my spirit is at home;
There strength and light and life are given me,
And full satisfaction.
Ah, that I might never depart from there!

389. Jesus to the Soul

I love you, O soul—I will be wholly yours.
I have bought and chosen you for My bride.
Turn all your love-power only into Me;
The creature has appearance—I am the true Being.

390. Whoever Looks to God Does Not Err

Would you walk purely and safely,
You must not look aside.
Let the still gaze of your spirit
Be sweetly fixed on God.
Let no fear confuse you—
He who walks so cannot err.
This simple attention
Sanctifies you and all your work.

391. Divine Chastity

He who would be Jesus' chaste bride
Must have no comfort on earth.
Desire must not enter in

Even in light, or comfort, or other gifts.
In God—and not in His treasures—
Must the chaste mind delight.

392. Love's Purgatory

Love is a fire that tolerates no dross,
That separates all selfhood from our soul.
Give its flames room and regard no pain—
It will at last become in you a life of joy.

393. What Is Melted Flows Easily into One

Through suffering the soul is softened and bowed,
Like wax melted and made pliant in fire,
Until at last God can flow into it and it into God,
And His grace will sweeten the pain of the cross.

394. Only One Breast Satisfies My Desire

No, creatures—none of you
Shall comfort me.
He who can turn into Jesus
Can do without you all.
Should it not be enough for me
To gaze upon the Bridegroom's face?

395. Soul, Put Nothing in the Way

Ask not at all
What happens here and there
In outward things.

You take in only images
That become a veil to you—
Not to press nakedly into God.

396. Love Makes One Not Notice

How—do you flee the cross? Enter into love,
And the cross will become to you a beloved messenger.

397. Sin Condemned by Sin

Before, I did sin with will and with delight;
Now must I suffer sin with pain and unwillingness.
This suffering indeed improves—yet, oh the bitter pain,
When sin must be condemned in us by sin!

398. All for All

Turn your love wholly out of all things
That outside God could bring you joy,
And rejoice in the Lord alone—
He will be to you more than all things.

399. Your Kingdom Come

My spirit is God's throne and precious heaven;
My flesh and outward part the footstool of His feet.
At my King's nod I bend heart and will;
Thus I live free and glad—the enemies must yield.

400. You See God When the Eye Is Closed

He who closes his eyes to himself and to all things
Beholds God in the light and lives in sure rest.

401. Our Shepherd-Office

I have a shepherd's charge: my desires and my thoughts
Are my sheep, on which my eye must always keep.
I hold them gathered into one, within the fence,
Lest they stray upon a foreign pasture.

402. The Best Guide

The Lord's eye leads me;
I must ever behold Him in a quiet spirit.
His nod shows me inwardly
How I should walk rightly and purely and safely.

403. My Love Is Crucified

Saying of St. Ignatius

Yes—my love is crucified and lifted high;
What profits me the whole world with honor, pleasure,
    treasures?
My hands are fast bound; I cannot take delight;
There is no fire in me but that which rises to the Father.

404. Do Not Cease Till the Grave

Keep your loins always girt with courage,
And yield to selfhood in nothing.
Yielded and loosed from all, you must turn to God;
In Him alone is what can truly gladden you.

405. What Does It Matter to You?

What is outside, whatever may occur,
You must behold like a stranger;
Remain untouched and undisturbed
With your Friend—turned into the spirit.

406. Rejoice in the Lord

Ah, dear soul—consider how good it is
That God is who He is, and acts as He acts!

407. Silence Is Best

To speak of God, O man, is good—when it is done well;
Yet he does better who speaks to God from the heart.
But best of all is when one can listen in silence
To what God Himself would say and teach us.

408. How One Becomes Strong

The spirit grows dim and weak when one indulges pleasure;
He who continually denies himself receives ever-new strength.

409. Walking in the Spirit

Lift up your spirit from within,
Gently above world, nature, and the senses,
And walk thus—loosed from all—
With God alone, content and glad.

410. My God and My All

Let God alone be your delight, your comfort, your friend, your treasure;
Let no creature have place within your heart!

411. God Calls—Enter the Little Chamber

God Himself is inwardly near you;
His drawing urges you there as well.
Who would not practice continually
To behold and love the Friend?

412. He Who Clings to Nothing Lives in Rest

Let go every creature—and yourself as well;
What God takes from you, surrender, and love Him purely and simply.
Who is thus stripped can rise freely in God,
Untouched by storms, living in blessed stillness.

413. He Who Would Have Good Days

He who would gladly live
In unshaken stillness and 'good days'
Must place his rest—whatever happens—
Only in God's will.

414. The Least—the Best

He who has light and gifts and accomplishes great things
Is not therefore more valued before God than others;
But he who stays turned inward, annihilated in humility—
Toward him God's heart and grace are most inclined.

415. Nature and Grace

Nature always seeks itself; grace seeks God alone.
See whether your mind and doing be stained or pure.

416. After Short Suffering Comes Eternal Joy

If God sends you a cross, embrace it willingly;
He who loves Jesus need not fear his cross.
The days of suffering will gladden you most
On that Day.

417. Through Everything—Aim Your Mind at God

What one suffers here and what one enjoys
Changes—and swiftly passes away;
Therefore do not delay over anything at all:
Direct your course nakedly toward God!

418. Remembrance of God

Let the heart's inward thoughts
Never wander, scattered, into outward things.
God is a light; whoever forgets Him
Is soon in danger and in sin.

419. My House Is Destroyed—So I Go Out

If you feel your misery, O soul, then go out of yourself;
Leave wholly your old, destroyed house.
If you can choose God Himself as your dwelling in the spirit,
You shall be eternally free of every load and torment.

420. The Cross Is a Burden While One Hates It

The cross is to you as you are to the cross:
If you are its enemy, it is hateful to you;
But when one embraces the cross and loves it,
The cross gives us God—and all grace.

421. Free—Yet Bound

Free from all things,
Be bound to God
With all the powers of love!
If you stand thus in truth,
Then you remain still and glad—
Alone and in your labors.

422. The Way to Solitude

Be wholly dead to creatures—
So your heart stays free of images
And becomes in spirit common with God;
Thus you are everywhere alone.

423. Farewell to All

Now depart, O creature—
My Creator only will I seek.
Away forever, all selfhoods:
I will wholly part from you.
God, the Pure One—refine me, till I am clean
In His eyes.
To Him I will yield myself eternally
And embrace Him only in the spirit.

424. Do Not Neglect the Best Duty

In all your doing—in writing and in reading—
Pause often a little and turn within.
Mark: God is near in the Ground; let Him be your Teacher,
That what you write and read may become in you power and substance.

425. In Sweet Familiarity

Remain quiet and of good courage—inwardly glad and small;
Let nothing enter you that wounds your sweet trust or troubles love,
Nothing that would darken the Ground—
But turn lovingly inward into your Friend's heart.
He who wills nothing but God alone
May be of good cheer in faith.

426. The Treasure in Earthen Vessels

Contempt, poverty, weakness, suffering
Cover here the radiance of Jesus' bride;
Yet soon the shell will part from the kernel—
Then shall she be seen in glory.
Faith's eye looks into eternity
And loves the cross, which only separates the dross.

427. A Glad Heart in Cross and Pain

The body nailed to the cross, the soul in inward suffering,
The spirit in God's hand—yielded, still, and glad;
Pressed down and yet content, sorrowful and yet rejoicing:
O fair Christian state—O soul, would you be so!

428. The Christian's School

The cross is the Christian's school; whoever would learn much in it
Let him, like a child, hold still before the great Teacher.

429. Love for the Cross

To praise the cross when it is far away,
Self-love can do as well;
To love the cross when one has it—
That only God's grace can do.

430. Xavier—What Did He Say?

'More yet!' cried Xavier when God sent him suffering;
'It is enough!' said he when grace refreshed him.
So bold am I not, for my love is small;
Yet if God sends greater strength, then let Him send greater pain!

431. Who Finds the Treasure? A Little Child Has It

Loosed from all and bare,
Innocent, small, and will-less
Must our soul be.
Reason never finds the pearl;
Only a naked child
Enters God's kingdom.

432. The Body—a Prison

The body on this earth
Ever weighs our spirit down;
It sits as one imprisoned.
Yet whoever loves the Lord, let him not be dismayed:
He will soon come home.
Soon the cord snaps in two;
Then the little bird can fly free
In God's air and swing.
Meanwhile it sings here
To the Lord with longing,
That it may succeed.

433. One Must Hate the Evil

The evil Adam-child still wants to be esteemed;
And if one prefers others, it soon is in pain.
Indeed one often makes oneself appear small, yet in the
    Ground believes it not—
And so robs the Highest Good, God Himself, of honor.

434. You Are Captive

Love binds us: O man, if your longing
Goes into world and creature, then it holds you captive.
Take my love wholly, O Jesus, into You,
That I may be forever only Your prisoner.

435. Self-Love and Love of God

He who seeks and loves himself
Lives pressed and becomes troubled;
He who loves God and forgets himself
Is free and light in spirit.

436. The Lord Is Good

The Lord is good in all His ways—
What does it matter about us and our condition?
Whatever God does with us, we must always cry out this
    word:
The Lord is good!

437. In the Fire Gold Is Tested

One thinks one loves God—and has not yet been tested.
One tastes this and that and thinks one loves well;
But he who feels neither grace nor comfort, neither God nor
    gifts,
And yet can still love—he loves as he ought.

438. O Great Grace—Who Has This!

God dwells in my Ground; therefore my whole being bows
And in sweet fear keeps silence in His nearness.
He anoints soul and spirit with inward, deep peace;
Thus I live will-less, detached from all.

439. Forget It Not!

You must hate yourself
And let God work you through and through,
And love firmly and purely;
Ever strive in all things
To please Him best—
Let this be your joy!

440. To Jesus! To Jesus!

A little ray passes by—turn your face to the sun.
A drop does not satisfy—run yourself to the spring.
You find the fountain of life only in your heart;
Turn your thirst inward from every creature.

441. Rule of Peace

Galatians 6:16

An untroubled, free disposition
That always thinks on God in love,
That entrusts itself to Him and His goodness,
Rejoices, sinks into Him,
And forgets all else besides—
Take this as your rule, wherever you are.

442. He Who Is Not Bound Soon Finds

The spirit is a weight that always inclines toward its Ground;
Its center is God, who touches and draws it.
Let go the creature that so easily binds it,
And it will sink of itself to the ground—
Where God is found within you.

443. Soon It Is Accomplished

After rain comes sunshine,
After cold and storms, summer days;
Joy follows pain,
Blessed rest follows cross and toil.
Here it is day, here it is night—
Soon we shall sing: It is finished.

444. Stay Quiet at Home

How unwilling we are to stay at home—
The thousand-skilled deceiver lures us out!
We think to do much good;
Yet by our doing we only harm.
We help when we rest in stillness
And allow ourselves to be undone by God.

445. Why Do You Live?

Our willing, our thinking,
Our acting and beginning—
What is not from God and unto God
Passes away like an empty dream.
Ah, we live almost in vain
Our brief span of life.
Die to yourself; live in God—
This alone must be your work here.

446. Soon, Soon!

A little while yet in misery,
Soon every burden ends;
A little while yet cross and distress,

Soon a blessed death refreshes.
A little while yet longing,
Soon you reach the goal;
Hold out just a little more—
Soon the spirit is at home.
A little, a little still,
Soon the Prince of Peace
Receives you into His peace-element
Forever, forever, without end.

447. Always at Home

God is always near me—at home or far away;
He ever thinks of me and gladly speaks with me.
No place confines Him, no place shuts Him out;
He who can dwell in God is everywhere at home.

448. Abandonment

If you cannot think for yourself,
Learn childlike to sink
Into the sea of God's will.
If you cannot guide your ship,
Let it sail by faith alone
And desire nothing but God.

449. Undismayed—Only Venture!

Fainthearted soul, be content—
Confident in God and detached.
Trust the Lord quietly and firmly;
Lie still before God in humility.
He will not deceive a poor child
Who relies on sheer grace alone.

450. Hard—and Yet Easy

How deep is our great corruption—
It costs bitter cross and dying
Before one becomes truly free and pure.
Yet whoever yields himself into God's hand,
Forgets himself and loves God alone,
May be redeemed even with ease.

451. A Naked Child Finds Everything

As a little child—unadorned and still—
Lay your naked Ground before God's eyes.
Let tongue, reason, desire, and will fall silent—
What does not such childlike simplicity teach and give us!

452. Stay Within the Fortress

Let all the powers of hell rage,
Let winds and seas storm—
Take no unrest upon yourself.
Let only your deepest will
Remain with God in inward, gentle stillness;
There the enemy cannot find you.

453. The Detached Cross-Bearer

I yield the outer man
To bitter pains of the cross;
The detached mind lies wholly still
In God's heart.
How strong and blessed is the man
Who can thus bear his suffering!

454. Turn the Mind Inward

Close the windows of your senses,
Else the spirit of the world will seize you.
Attend to God's inward drawing,
Which gladly gathers you.
He Himself leads us in His ways—
But hear how you must walk:
Straight against self-will—
Thus every sensual desire dies.

455. Uprightness

Uprightness: to harbor nothing against God,
Uprightness toward God alone.
Such a Ground gives firmness in dark ways,
Gives courage—but it must be thorough.
With this Ground one must yield to God
And let Him lead as He wills,
Through mountain and valley, cross and death to life;
As much as you can—remain inward, small, and still.

456. It Ever Draws Shorter

The pilgrim's path is full of hardship,
Yet the way is no longer far.
God strengthens in the meantime;
The weary pilgrim will rest at home
In the Father's bosom
And forget all suffering.

457. Good, Better, Best

To do the Lord's will is good and right;
Better still is to do it willingly;
But to do it from the heart and in purity—
This, truly, is the very best.

458. Fair, Fairer, Fairest

It is fair to separate one's heart from all things;
Fairer still, to suffer according to God's will.
He who wills nothing, is nothing, has nothing, can do nothing—
That one is before God the fairest of all.

459. Fear, Faith, Love

He who fears God hates sin,
Keeps what is right,
And stands afar as a servant.
He who believes God finds grace,
Becomes pure and devout,
And is God's friend.
He who loves God yields himself
As a child
And finds his Father near.
This child fears, trusts, loves,
Acts, suffers, and is still—
As God, his Father, wills.

460. Short Way to Holiness

Forget, as far as you are able,
Yourself and your sins,
And become childlike in spirit with God alone;
Thus you may easily find God and His grace—
Even the greatest sinner may quickly become holy.

461. 'Therefore I Shall Not Be Moved'

God, who fills heaven and earth,
Be near you also in your thoughts.
This quiet being stills
When we waver and grow faint;
God, gently beheld in spirit,
Makes the soul steadfast and unshaken.

462. Inward Shortening of Time

An eye withdrawn from all,
Ever turned toward God;
A heart detached,
Known by God in the spirit,
That inwardly embraces Him
With silent love—
This is my pastime,
In which I daily exercise myself.

463. God Helps the Good Will

Who cannot yet become fully free
Yet wills it from the heart,
The Lord makes pleasure turn to burden
And what he loves into pain.

He takes away this and that,
Until at last He takes all—
Blessed is he who lets God act
And gives Him everything.

464. 'Come unto Me, You Weary'

Jesus gladly makes Himself near—
Why then be timid?
Think: a rich man and a poor,
A sinner and a Savior—
Your sin and Jesus' blood
Belong well together.

465. Pain Drives the Soul Inward to God

The Lord blocks my path with thorns;
The dear cross presses me so I can scarcely move.
Hear, O soul, how bitterness may be sweetened:
Out of all things, turn into God—
There you find wide room.

466. Halt! Halt!

How the blind man runs,
As though he had lost his senses!
Ah, run not so fast—
You are running toward eternity.
Think: in this brief moment of grace
A soul may be lost—or won.

467. Live Surrendered to God

From all things turn your spirit toward God alone
And yield yourself childlike forever into His hands.
As He works, be still, content, and will-less;
Love the Father only
And remain in His bosom.

468. Look to Jesus

Forget yourself, O sinner, with all your sins,
And look only upon Jesus—you shall find grace.
Go on thus: look at Jesus and nothing else;
Thus even the greatest sinner becomes a child of light.

469. Jesus to the Soul

Child, empty your heart
And hold it open in stillness;
I will flow into it
And fill your vessel.

470. Stillness Gives Strength

A still spirit despises
Satan's craft and power;
With confident courage
It conquers flesh and blood.
The world and all its ways
It easily laughs at,
Because it trusts in God,
Whom it beholds by faith.

471. The Best Mirror

You look in the mirror,
Would gladly be fair,
Yet remain a beast,
Stained with sin.
I mirror myself in God—
He looks into me.
Shall even a speck of dust
Hide itself from the purest light?

472. Praying Without Ceasing

Once I chose place and time
For prayer and solitude;
Now I pray always in silent intent,
Now I am solitary wherever I am.

473. Pleasure Without Burden

What pleasure craves today,
Tomorrow it abandons;
But look upon and love God—
Of Him you shall never tire.
Ask the seraphim,
After thousands of years,
With what they have filled their time so long.

474. Evening Stillness

Lovely, dark, gentle, and still
Is the sweet hour of evening;
Would that my soul's Ground and will

Might always so remain.
God's presence alone
Makes this possible.

475. Beating the Air

You pray fervently, it seems;
You complain, ask, desire much;
You threaten your foe—
Yet only strike at air.
Give desire and will wholly captive,
Else victory is never won.

476. The Best Love

He who loves and wants much
Loves himself and God's gifts.
To love with much comfort and light
Is not the best love.
Love God in bare faith;
Let all else be taken from you—
Even if God Himself seems to withdraw—
Love, and lose yourself for God.

477. It Always Works Out

Our resolve and our thinking
Must be guided by the Father's will;
If it does not go as we wish,
God's will, instead of all else,
Can bring me joy and peace—
So that I remain content.

478. Cover the Fire

Let love, withdrawn from all,
Embrace God in inward, silent peace.
Remain within yourself, admit nothing else—
This tender fire must be covered.

479. Fruitful Stillness

Stillness is not idleness:
When the eye beholds God alone
And yields to His working,
Ah—such loving attention
Is before God a great work.

480. The Heart with the Treasure

When I stand at work,
Eat, drink, sit, or walk,
Ah—the heart is elsewhere,
Untouched and inwardly glad.
Only in spirit, one with God—
There must my dwelling be.

481. 'Yes, Father!'

Matthew 11:26

Without my own choosing or resisting,
I yield myself to all His will;
Ever saying yes, and never no—
Thus one is freed from every pain.

Glad and still at God's least sign,
The will must quickly sink away
And call good all that God both wills and does.

482. Healing Through Enemies

My enemy is truly my friend:
He torments the self-will
With which, alas, I myself am plagued.

483. Let It Go

Whoever takes what is yours
Takes your burden as well.
You shall not find rest
Until you have nothing of your own.

484. The Carefree Child

I am a child—I cannot worry;
Therefore I give myself to the Mother
And rest hidden in her bosom
In quiet, surrendered childlikeness.
To look back or think ahead
Would only wound my heart in vain

485. Like a Beast, O Lord, With You

Psalm 73:22

I must be ready to suffer;
A beast must bear its load,
And I the Lord's yoke.

My God, I am Your simple beast—
Lay on Your cross; I will carry it for You
And yet remain near You.

486. The Cautious Pilgrim

A pilgrim weary from the road
Sits down awhile in quiet rest;
So I return from time to time in spirit
To my sweet repose—
Thus I journey on,
Yet live at home with the Father.

487. Heroic Love

He who is angered by his foe
Is not yet a man;
A hero is one
Who can also love his enemies.

488. The Inward Life

Let go of all externals,
Let everything else fall away;
Your spirit must be free, still, unformed.
Let there be no will in you
Save God's good pleasure—
Thus live with the heart's Beloved
In the inner chamber.

489. 'Martha, Martha!'

Ah Martha, leave your anxious care
And cease your restless labor!
Your guardian, Jesus, still lives—
So wise, so strong, so good.
Let Him manage your affairs;
Your only care: to keep Him company in stillness.

490. Unwearying

Climb yet a little higher,
Gently out of yourself and all things;
Surely the narrow way of the cross
Will bring you home to God.
Climb yet a little higher—
Soon it will be done.

491. 'Man, You Dream!'

Who does not remain with God in the heart
And spend his time with Him
Has squandered his life—
As though he had been dreaming.

492. Everything for the One

Ah, all here is vanity;
Man, one thing alone is needful.
Turn wholly away from all else—
You take only one thing to the grave.

493. Untouched and God-Surrendered

In Christ's cross lie rest, comfort, and breadth,
Where the spirit remains detached
From hope and fear, from pain and joy,
From self and all the world.
When no such storm tosses you anymore,
The surrendered Ground is moved by God alone.

494. Love of Friends and Enemies

Cross, burden, and mockery of foes
Drive us nearer to God;
Favor, honor, and friends' praise
Steal time and strength and peace.
Love friend and enemy alike—
Only depart not from your inner Ground.

495. Love That Draws

God's love is my magnet:
It draws me gently yet powerfully,
So that my spirit moves into God's being—
Moving and running, yet not busy.
Working-less and will-less,
It sinks of itself into God's bosom.

496. 'Here Is the Place'

Now you are here, now there,
And nowhere truly where you should be.
Let all your here and there disappear—
Only here find you your home.

497. Jesus to the Soul

You often come to Me,
Yet never alone;
Thus I cannot speak freely with you.
A will, an image, a form disturbs our solitude,
So I cannot speak, and you cannot hear.
Come without yourself, my child—
Then we shall be truly alone.

498. Without Self-Reflection

You must not look upon yourself
If you would walk securely;
Your eye must be clear and single.
Look childlike upon God alone in all things
And never glance back
Into self-will.

499. Jesus to the Soul

Be still, dear child—the house is Mine.
Clear out your heart and everything within;
Sit down and look on gently
At what I am and do inside.

500. 'My Shadow Made Me Think Thus'

In Paradise my body
Cast no shadow at all;
Here it lives in cross and shame,
A mere life of shadows.

Though this shadow-body breaks apart,
I shall inherit a nobler dwelling,
Where, filled with God's light,
I shall shine forever without shadow.

501. At the Bloodletting

They draw my blood—
If God so wills, it is well with me.
Yet if I am to be truly healed, and healing please God,
Then only Jesus' blood must course
Through heart and veins.
O Jesus, let this pure, sweet life of love
Fill my breast;
Then gladly—yes, I swear it—I will joyfully
Offer even the final drop for You.

502. Jesus to the Soul

I long to raise the spirit—
Let it be wholly yielded to Me,
Still, free, intimate, without self-will,
Seeking life in no created thing;
Then it shall find life
In My bosom.

503. Grace Is Hard to Receive

It is truly not easy to be saved by grace—
To be righteous in Christ and not in oneself.
This is the highest art and noblest state on earth:
To trust wholly in God alone,
Stripped of every support.

504. The Practice of a Child

To think of Jesus,
To sink into Him,
Without complaint or offense;
To be childlike,
To give oneself wholly to Him with delight,
To be guided
From Jesus' breast.

505. Be Child-Minded

On God's paths
One must not investigate or calculate.
Reason—be still, dumb, and blind!
Whether stripped or refreshed,
What comes is sent by God.
Look to the Mother; remain a child.

506. As with God Alone

Accept whatever comes from God as good,
Cling to Him and adapt yourself to Him,
Commit yourself and all things to God;
Think more of God than of yourself as you go.
O sweet God—whoever delights You
Lies content with You even in misery.

507. Watch and Pray

Attend inwardly to God's call
And follow simply, rightly, faithfully;
Draw strength from Jesus through prayer

And gladly be alone with Him.
Thus Jesus teaches you God's will
And Himself fulfills it in you.

508. Come and See

Whoever does not follow Jesus
Remains without light.
One may hear the sound—
But whoever does not strive to live as Jesus lived
Never truly grasps His teaching.

509. 'Behold, I Am with You'

The Lord is near and wills
To quiet you by His nearness.
Let your heart and all desire
Gently turn toward Him;
Give Him true room in your depths
As your one and only treasure.

510. The Pilgrim's Guidepost

If you wish to travel, hear how you must go:
In the world and in sin there is no good road.
Turn toward the wilderness,
Past all created things;
Pass through reason and the senses—
Do not linger there.
Go deeper downward
Through self-denial into the heart.
Ignore what lies to either side;
Look only forward, gently and still.
Never walk alone—
Let Jesus be your guide.

Strict walking is true abiding;
Stillness is the swiftest haste.
One easily strays by light—
Follow blindly, and you will not err.
If you walk this narrow path,
Many crosses will appear.
The way of the cross is lonely, deep,
Narrow, barren, desolate—
Yet whoever dares
May taste honey even in the desert.
Here and there one is nourished,
Then sent onward again.
When the great desert comes—
Remain faithful to the Guide.
If it is dark, dry, and long,
Do not be afraid:
When you arrive there,
You are near your homeland.

511. The Cautious Helmsman

God looks into me,
And I look only to Him;
My rudder and compass are nothing else.
If this holds,
My little ship sails safely,
Though wind and waves storm.
Doubt and unfaithfulness
Make me look at myself—
Then I begin to sink.
But Jesus, who loves me,
Reaches out His hand again.
Ah, if only I could stand firm
And gaze on Him without turning aside!

512. A Child's Farewell

    Children, do not call this a parting—
    Fatherland and Father remain near.
    Seek me in the Spirit; there we meet.
    Only go deeper inward—
    God awaits us there.

513. The Joyful Sabbath

    When human will
    And self-activity grow still,
    Then God can work and enliven the depths;
    There freedom and purity are given.

514. Blessed Eternity

    Into the still Now
    I sink with deep intimacy,
    My only good, into You—
    Into the Ground of the soul.
    There, beyond time and place,
    Far from self and creature,
    I live content with You alone.

515. The Gathering

    Where shall thought, desire, and mind go?
    Gather what is scattered in multiplicity;
    Let the powers of love be gently drawn
    Toward your God at eternity's point.
    Let go of all—
    There you will find the One,
    The only thing necessary and sufficient.

516. Be Still Before the Lord

As a blank page lies beneath the writer's hand,
So must you surrender yourself—
Image-free, without resistance.
Through letting go, waiting, and suffering
God prepares us best.

517. Our One Task

Out of love for the Highest Good
Renounce self, pleasure, and will;
With gentle, quiet courage
Let this be your work and delight:
To walk always as a child
In the presence of God the Father.
If I wrote a thousand pages,
I would remain with this one thing.

518. Many Loved Ones, One Beloved

Friends of God, I love you dearly,
Yet I love one Friend more.
When He wills to walk with me alone,
You—and even what is dearest—remain outside.
O sweet solitude, where all fades gently away,
Where the eye finds nothing
And the heart loves nothing
But the Highest Good alone.

519. Flee the Tumult

The spirit must gently withdraw,
Released from time and place,
Into the still land of eternity,
Where no noise can reach it.
What is spoken and done outside
Does not concern you.

520. The Kingdom of God Is Within You

Close your eyes, sink from yourself to the Ground—
Released, still, naked in the present Now.
Like a child, you will find right where you are
The inner kingdom: God Himself and His rest.

521. Who Harms You?

Whoever opposes you does you no real harm;
He only fights your true enemy—
Your own self-will.

522. If I Am Right, All Is Right

Never blame what happens outside you;
Do not complain of times, world, devil, or people.
Your own unbent heart, turned from God,
Is the bitter source of unrest and pain.
Let God make that heart good and holy—
Then even the cross becomes heaven on earth.

523. Against the Fever of Greed

> Greed—the universal fever—
> Drinks much and thirsts more, yet remains sick.
> Whoever has God overflows
> And drinks even as he gives drink to others.

524. Against Violent Headache

> Headache clouds the mind when severe;
> Self-love causes similar pain.
> You can see the fool in others—
> Seeing God and stepping back heals you.

525. The Wicked Debtor

> You boldly demand patience from others—
> Do you not incur debt yourself?
> Learn to think of repayment as well.
> Should one forgive you both principal and interest?

526. Childlike Faithfulness, Childlike Freedom

> Be exact and faithful in what lies before you
> For love of the Heart-God to whom you belong.
> Forget past and future—the more childlike, the better.
> Naked, small, trusting, still—
> Abandon yourself to the Father.

527. 'Ah, If Only!'

Ah, if only—if only
My heart were empty of all!
The world is too poor for me;
Nothing anywhere satisfies.
I cannot rest in gifts—
I must have the Giver.
Ah, if only—if only
I were empty of all!

528. Not Here, Not There—Within

Seek here, seek there—you remain in misery.
Only One can quiet you,
And that One is not far:
Within you.
God Himself longs
To gather and fill you.

529. The Best Defense

My poor heart, consecrated as God's city of peace,
Has a strong fortress in its depths—the name Jesus.
The enemies rage and besiege it,
Launching poisoned arrows day and night.
I do not rush out to fight—
I shut myself in and remain still in God.
Then no storm can harm me.

530. Go Inward and Be Still

Turn inward, human soul—
There shines the sun of grace.
God offers you His heart, His life, His light, His joy.
You block the sun with countless 'beautiful' things.
You think, will, and act—
Be silent before God; let Him act.
Still your cloudy little waters;
Otherwise the sun cannot shine within.

531. Obedience Is Better Than Sacrifice

Do not choose your own piety.
Learn to give heart and will truly to God
And live surrendered to His slightest sign.

532. The Hero

A still, confident heart
In want, distress, and pain,
Given eternally to God
In life and in death—
Where is such a hero
To be found on earth?

533. I Care for Myself

What concerns me how others act
Or how they treat me?
If I act rightly, keep watch,
Grow small and become clean—

Let others do as they may.
God gives, God governs—
I love the Man.

534. The Heavenly Calling

Heaven calls—away, flesh; away, earth!
My call is to become heavenly.
My God is here; I bow.
I offer all—my dearest.
Be still, my own willing, acting, thinking;
Lord, speak—
I will be silent to You.

535. He Will Come

How long Simeon waited
Before holding the Child!
I grow weary of waiting,
I sigh, I seek, I grow faint.
No—I remain faithful.
I let the Faithful act,
Even if I must grow old like Simeon.

536. The Sweetest Judgment

The only sweetness on the pilgrim road,
The sweetest thing in the homeland,
Is Jesus alone.
Who tastes only Jesus,
Finds the feast prepared in the Spirit.
Empty yourself—come in—
Sit down.

537. Little Child, Come

You grieve endlessly and remain miserable—
Believe it: God's mother-heart is near within you.
Lean gently inward; ignore the misery.
The Mother hears and sees
Even behind closed doors.

538. Let the Surrender Stand

One cannot surrender too firmly
To what one wishes to be forever.
I have spoken—and never regretted it:
My heart and life are Yours, Jesus.
Here again is my hand;
Set Your seal upon it.

539. The Wise Little Bee

From every devout soul I gather what nourishes me;
I seek no fault—good alone is my food.
Many flowers confuse no bee:
It seeks only sweetness, not poison or display.

540. Do Not Sow into the Wind

If the outer does not serve the inner
And the inner does not flower outward,
One works much and accomplishes little.
Truth, life, and anointing
Are found by the heart-child
Who celebrates God inwardly.

541. Is There No Physician in Israel?

You worry and weaken yourself—
Yet God is near,
Loves you more than you know.
Turn inward like a child;
He waits for you.
Live quietly for Him and give yourself fully.
Then His grace and tender peace will shape you.

542. The Straight Path

God is nearer than breath—
Do not seek Him far away.
He is a God of the heart.
Turn back—turn inward—He alone is enough.
Let Him act freely with you and your affairs;
Do not look at yourself or your works.

543. Where Nothing Is Seen, God Makes It Beautiful

I delight in the beauty of others
And blush at my own defects.
God delights in this seeing and says:
Because you are naked, take My beauty—
But take it without grasping,
And come without shame.

544. I Build on the Rock Alone

How quietly the child of light walks in darkness,
Leaning only on its Friend.
Light and feeling fade like flowers—
God and faith alone stand firm.

545. The Best Focus

Self-love hides beneath humility,
Thinking always of self.
If you would know true peace,
Think of God with love and trust.

546. Seek My God Alone

Do not divide the stream of pure desire—
It loses force and sinks into sand.
Give all desire to God,
And He gives Himself freely to you.

547. Looking Around Confuses; Looking to God Does Not

One praises me, another condemns me;
My guiding star is God alone.
Who sees Him forgets self
And walks blessed and free.

548. Where Shall I Go to Church?

You seek the temple far away—
Yet God is near.
Wherever one seeks God, honors Him,
And beholds Him—
There is the church.

549. Empty and Near

Can you behold the death of your spirit without tears?
Believe it: God's well is full.
When Hagar's jar was empty,
She found the nearby spring.

550. Christian Wisdom

My eye looks to God and truth—
Not to what I am or how I am treated.
God is enough for the one
Who walks before Him.

551. It Comes Down to One Thing

If I do not have within me
The favor of the greatest Friend,
Then a thousand comforts outside me
Hardly console at all.
And enemies all around me cannot truly harm me either,
If my Friend—near within—speaks me satisfied.

552. The Old Adam's Trick

The worst inherited skill I know
Is our self-excusing.
True children of the heart
Easily and blindly count themselves
Guilty sinners.

553. Sweetness from Bitterness

Ah, pray—draw close—learn to accept sweetly
When friends and foes exercise you
And often press you painfully.
You still live—so it hurts; God uses them, therefore love.
You do not think—do not believe—how they guard you
And make you devout.

554. God in You, God in Everything

God is near within,
God is at every boundary;
In everything clear to see,
In everything sweet and beautiful,
In everything worthy of love—
All that a heart could want.
In everything I worship and yield myself to His hands.
My blessedness, my one concern,
Is God—not me, not creature.

555. The Happy Hermit

Only that one lives free and joyful
Who lives alone with God—
Indeed in the world, yet foreign to it,
And inwardly hovering above it.
The crowd itself doesn't prevent solitude;
Whatever your heart lets in
Stays with you wherever you are.

556. Jesus Says: Abide in Me!

People say: 'So it must be—leaves, blossoms, fruit.'
Right—then seek and draw the sap
That accomplishes it in you.
No green branch can endure
In a jar or in your hand;
Stand on the root—
Then it stays truly beautiful.

557. The Child on the Lead

Inward, my child—do not dare it alone;
Let the Father's hand lead, hold, and carry you.
A child of the heart is strong
When it stays near the Heart;
Otherwise it is more foolish and weaker
Than many a 'letter-Christian.'

558. On Forgetting the Self

To forget yourself
And spend your time on things that are nothing—
Person, notice that folly!
To forget yourself and teach others—
Hardly converted, converting the world—
That is poor and risky work.
To forget yourself by seeing Jesus,
To disregard yourself and exalt God—
Only this gives courage and strength.

559. It Is Good to Be Here

What has happened to me—where have I been led?
What new world has taken me in!
My spirit feels the deepest stillness in its Ground;
I have entered paradise—and it has entered me.
My once-oppressed spirit now has wide room;
It breathes fresh air and rises gently.
How lively it looks—once hardly moving—
Now free, living in the element of purest joy.
Luke 9:36: 'And they kept silent.'

560. The Origin of Evil

No—You essential Good,
Evil cannot come from You.
Whoever withdraws love from You
And does his own will—
He is the one who makes sin,
Who brings himself distress and pain,
Who builds hell in his own heart.
Whoever leaves the light is in the night.
I am Your little ray, my Sun—

Let me never be separated from You,
So I remain free from sin and suffering
And live in the delight of Your light!

561. Sin, the Cause of All Suffering

Person, take it deep into your heart:
To leave God is bitter.
Confess it rightly, give God the honor,
And do not be foolish anymore.
Let not the serpent deceive you—
Sin is a short, false pleasure.
Small lust is followed by heavy burden;
Who sins hates himself.
Lord, let me cling to You in the cross!
Even if sin could give me heaven
And Your love could bring such pain,
Still I would not choose to be a sinner.

562. Encouragement to Fight

Who could sleep with so many enemies
And sit secure?
If you want to live, take up weapons
And gird yourself for battle.
Leave world and every load behind—
Honor, rank, pleasure, money, goods.
Let neither lust nor fear bind you
Or break your heroic courage.
Guard your heart and every sense;
Spare not your dearest.
Cling unwaveringly to Jesus within
Until all enemies' power is defeated!

563. Patient Purifying of the Sensory Part

So the Lord removes all supports
On which our senses lean,
When comfort, light, and strength grow cold
And only misery is felt.

Then I feel what I am and can do;
Then I learn true surrender to God—
To live in spirit and dark faith
On that beautiful path of the cross.

Lord, teach me to trust only You,
To dare everything with You in faith,
Not to yield or despair in the cross,
And to wait on You patiently.

564. Patient Purifying of the Spirit

As soon as fire's heat finds green wood,
It draws out the sap and drives out strength;
It blackens the bark, the flame ignites,
And burns through and through until nothing remains—
Then it glows beautifully and still.
So it is in the heart
When one yields unconditionally to love's discipline.
This fire purifies us through strange pains
And often depresses us again and again, even toward death.
Yet it is only love—so it must deal with us,
Burning away whatever in the depths resists it.
Give its flame room, and it will transform you
Until you are wholly one with God,
And God alone lives in you.

565. I Will Accept the Healing Cup

No—the cross is no burden
Except to the soul that hates it.
Whoever embraces it in love
And can surrender childlike to God
May, in the cross's pain,
Be inwardly still and joyful.

Self-will—complain;
Murmur, senses and nature!
You must complain, you must die,
If the spirit is not to perish.
The cross is good and dear and light
Because it is God's love reaching us.

566. Glorious Fruits of Suffering

O tree of the cross, full of beautiful fruit—
More desirable to behold
And more heart-refreshing to taste
Than that tree in paradise
By which Eve was deceived
With a deadly, false delight!

The cross tastes bitter in the mouth,
Yet it heals from such death.
It is good to eat from the tree of the cross—
May I never forget it!
This tree makes one wise and glad and free;
Who would not eat without fear?

567. Blessed End of Suffering

Who would not suffer here on earth?
A small weight of cross in this short time
Will there be repaid
With a thousand weights of joy in eternity!
Where are those now
Who lived a few years here in empty pleasure?
And those who bore cross and pain—
Where have they gone?
They have forgotten all distress;
They adorn God's throne
With crowns of glory and white robes;
The blessedness is immeasurable.

568. The Echo and Answering Echo of Love

Notice what love wants:
To become a whole offering
On earth.
Only be still under its pull;
Give yourself captive to love
In unadulterated faithfulness.
Let this inward longing
Be your constant echo:
To become a whole offering
On earth.

569. Path to Illumination

You single, pure Light—cure of the soul's blindness—
Who teaches all truth if I only bow:
Naked and blind
Like a child
Who knows nothing and wants to know nothing,

And so remain still before You in my depths.
Then Your face gives me
Sufficient light—
Sufficient light—though I see only One thing;
Yet in that One I easily understand all.
So it is not 'many things,' not images, but truth;
And everything leads me straight into the One clarity.

570. Dark Surrender of Faith

Now my Friend remains within, in His inner chamber;
What He is there, what He does there,
I do not seek to see or know.
My seeing makes me unfit and wretched for seeing.
I cannot go in; I must keep watch at the little door—
Content with His doing, I let Him go on.
Yet within I am poor and bare;
The dryness and darkness are great.
Still I must not weep or complain,
Not look around, not fear, not ask:
'Where am I? Is this the right path?'
I live on God's grace.
The rudder is no longer in my hand;
God knows where my little ship will find land.
Yet I am content even in this pain—
Surrender now must be without limits.

571. Blessed Are Those Who Dwell in Your House

Day and night I practice my inner priesthood.
My heart would give God everything—
Sweet and sour, death and life.
I do it gladly, yet remain always silent.
My speaking is a sweet silence;
My doing, a gentle, contented bowing.

I tell the Lord very much
Though the tongue seems idle.
I do this day and night
And do not tire of it.

572. With the Betrothed One Comes Too Late

Go, vain world—
Lure, praise, blame—
You come too late. I will not glance back
At your fantasies.
I have already given my blooming youth
To the fairest Friend.
He bought my heart, sought it, found it,
And bound it to His heart and yoke.
Him I may name
And freely confess:
He is Jesus Christ,
Forever my treasure, my salvation, my all.

573. You Hide Them Secretly

Psalm 31:20

Out—out
Of this strange house!
Let your spirit turn inward to eternity;
Let that be from now on
Your nest, your refuge,
So the world and self-will do not disturb you.
Let God's heart alone
Be your quiet chamber;
Then you have rest in all things,
Though the body still must wander here and there.

574. The School of Wisdom

Truly learned is the one
Who desires nothing for himself,
Who wants to be nothing in all things,
Who does not even want to please himself,
Who finds nothing in himself
Except that, like a little child,
He wants to know nothing, think nothing—
Only to sink into his nothingness.
O beautiful Nothing—
Fullness of all light,
Sun of clarity,
Fountain of pure truth,
Hidden little corner,
So unimpressive, so small—
Who would think, poor little house,
That you would grant us true wisdom?

575. Inside, They Call You

Inward, inward,
Little eye of the soul—
Gently restrain the urge of the senses.
Your dearest Friend is inside you;
Look—He wants you entirely.
He gathers heart and mind and what was scattered.
Who would not sink inward
And yield to love's guidance?
Completely still and silent—
The Lord is there in His sanctuary.
Even amid outward dealings and works,
Let this inward look strengthen the quiet mind;
And after the work, it goes again, gently:
Inward, inward.

576. Oh, If We Were There!

There it is beautiful—
Where thousands of little flames stand,
Shining forever, sweet and gentle;
There they no longer shine in darkness—
They burn as eternal adornment
Before God's throne always.
A gentle oil streams from Jesus' heart
That makes the candles of blessed spirits bright and glad.
Cross, fear, and every torment of suffering,
All darkness itself,
Are swallowed up in the light of delight
That has penetrated spirit, soul, and body forever.
There the mouths of infants
Proclaim the Highest's praise and wonders;
Purest innocence reigns;
The host of children rejoices sweetly.
One will see the eternal Light in light:
There it is beautiful!

577. The Speck in the Sun

Where do I find myself?
How great is God—how small am I!
What is a dust-speck
In bright sunlight?
How could I not forget myself and all things,
Since I live and float in the immeasurable Being?
You, Being of Love, are nearer to me than I am to myself;
So I think only of You and yield myself to You.
Swallow up what is mine entirely, O Sun—
Let the air of Your love be my delight,
The light of Your nearness my sunshine,
And my soul Your little dust-speck.

578. A Riddle

I saw three different children nursing.
One used mouth, ears, and eyes;
It asked and spoke cleverly
Of mother, breast, and milk—
And amid childlike delight
It nursed now and then, but never enough.
Another used its mouth to nurse,
Its ears while nursing to hear
What beautiful things the mother taught;
It did not need eyes for either—
It did not look around for breast or mother;
Smiling, it became full, taught, and devout.
The third, a very little child,
Needed only its mouth to nurse;
It neither looked nor listened when called.
Yet somehow (I don't know how) it must have known
The mother, whom it could not name.
She spoke—it laughed; she sang—it slept.
Now guess—who can—
Not for quarrel but for joy:
Name and choose for yourself
The wisest of the three.

579. For a Birthday

You gave me, Lord, the breath of life;
You gave me grace and strength and much besides.
If I have not given it to You, I have it all in vain;
So give it to me today anew for this new year.
Ah, stay with Your little band of children—
Evening comes; the devout grow fewer.
If You will that I still wander in this tent,
Make me light and salt among them.

580. Still for a Birthday

As I was—
Sixty years—
And looked back,
Seeing neglect and wasted time,
I thought: 'Shame—we humans dream!'
Have I not learned enough in so many years
That world and self do not satisfy?
Overfull—so I spit it out.
I want to rise from this foreign life
Into the coming one;
Only there is my spirit at home.

581. Reply to a Birthday Wish

You praise God for my years at the new year
And wish me fresh strength and blessing.
So be it.
For myself, one year—one day—would be too long;
And yet the longest time is too short
For God's praise and thanks.
Who knows this Being, for him
Praise is life; friendship is all honor;
Light is the robe of glory;
Will is food; service is blessedness.
But one is not satisfied here—eternity will give it.
The antechamber of that eternity
Is spiritual detachment:
There God closes our little eyes,
And one has everything in a single Now.

582. For the New Year

May God anoint us for the new year
With new pilgrim-strength—
For outward going and inwardness
And for the affairs of the Kingdom.
In the world but not of the world,
We cry outward toward home,
And in God—with every step—
We rejoice in one another.

583. Wish for a Jubilee Year

Exodus 21:5–6; Leviticus 25:10–13; Deuteronomy 15:17

In this jubilee year
May God grant what is real
And end slavery:
That we be forever willing servants
To the true Lord—
Our ear bored through at the doorpost—
Servants who nevertheless, in the house, live as children,
Freed by the Son and recognized as free.
So may our inheritance—
Whether we live or die—
Be fully turned toward us again.
Let us keep a sabbath year,
Let You, Father, rule;
May Your gentle sign govern us always—
Without sowing and without worrying,
Without yesterday and without tomorrow—
To die to ourselves and to celebrate You.

584. The Conclusion

Good reading often helps; good writing is also good—
Yet these are only images until one experiences and does them.
I leave the images and turn to the reality.
Reader, do the same.
This is the end of reading.

Later Gleanings

585. Harp-Playing Sanctified to God

To You, God, I bring heart and songs
So that I never sing in vain:
Let devotion's incense burn through Your sweet nearness;
Make Yourself great in me and make me small in heart.
Let my will tune itself gently to Your will;
Let my inmost being seek and intend You simply.
So my song honors You;
So my soul finds You sweet.

586. True Godliness, or True Worship

(1 Timothy 4:8)

Who fears God, believes, and loves,
Who serves Him rightly and gives Him honor—
This is true godliness.
Fear remains standing in the outer court
And bows from a distance;
It strikes the breast in sorrow and repentance,
Avoids what is evil, turns itself toward the good,
And strives for cleansing from dead works.
Faith enters the Holy Place
And ascends upward in prayer,

Sprinkled with the blood of Jesus like the altar of incense;
There Christ Himself gives the spirit bread and life,
And the illuminating light makes all truth clear.
Pure love may enter the Most Holy Place,
Where God dwells in deep darkness,
Resting in the silent spirit;
Who is thus united may worship the Godhead itself,
Embrace and behold it, as the cherubim do.
Let this be your worship.
In these three practices
Father, Son, and Spirit are rightly and purely honored.
All hypocrisy is useless.
Whoever can live this
May truly be godly—
And in God, truly blessed.

587. Do Not Strive After High Things

The heights of reason, its finest structure of skill,
Resemble a crumbling wall—
So lofty, so full of danger—
On which one climbs with effort and then suddenly falls.
Look at the fearful collapse!
People marvel at it.
There a daring man races out into the open field
Mounted on a wild beast,
Despising bridle and reins—
An image of false freedom.
Should that not be dangerous?
The same is seen in the heights of the spirit:
Observe the subtlety—
How on the pinnacle of the temple
One stands in peril, not far from Satan himself.
You who strive after wisdom,
Do not strive after high things.
Wisdom came down into the lowly;

She became a little child.
You will never be wise nor exalted
Unless you are willing to become small.
Come, let yourself be brought to Jesus as a child,
Let your school be the heart—
Enter there in prayer.
Attend to Jesus' teaching;
Let Him be your master.
See how His word and His Spirit
Give the lessons,
Sweeter than honeycomb
To the one who loves the Teacher.
The first letter of this lesson is called:
Be gladly unknown.

588. The Little Pearl

Praise greatly the heavy burden of iron if you will;
To me, one small pearl is worth far more.

589. The Most Excellent Way of Love

Strive all of you for the greatest gifts—
I desire only pure love.
The love of the Friend
Is the seal upon my heart;
The love of the brethren
Is the mirror of my walk.

590. The Name Jesus

May the sweet name Jesus
Be eternally sweet to you and daily renewed—
Strong for loving,
Strong for suffering,
And powerfully at work for perfection.

591. Love for Love

'Love's play of love
Is fair and great and manifold
In hearts set apart.
Whoever gives himself to Love
Is loved by Love
With a thousand loving wounds.'
Reason does not comprehend
What Love speaks here;
Yet these are no childish things.
Whoever reads and considers this
With inward attention
May be set aflame.

592. Sink as a Little Child into Sweet Grace

Sweet or bitter,
Joy or sorrow—
All is good that Jesus does.
Only remain lying
In the cradle,
And entrust yourself
To His care.

593. Surrender

Surrender is easy
After it has taken place,
But hard and heavy
Before it is fully born.
Whoever can wholly yield
His own right to God
Finally conquers
And overcomes even nature itself.

594. Do Not Fear, Little Flock

Poor Zion,
God is your reward;
Only remain faithful to Him.
Be patient,
Live innocently
Before the world,
And speak freely.

595. We Must Die — and We Will Die

If we must suffer out of necessity,
Then let us suffer all the way to death.

596. On a Birthday

Eight-and-thirty years ago
I entered into misery;
Praise be to God for breath and heart
And grace and a Father's care.
Yet I am rightly ashamed
When I consider it well:

Eight-and-thirty years—
And still not holy.
Lord, let the small remainder
Of my moments
Be wholly and unwaveringly devoted to You alone.
I must live for You,
Or else take me from the earth
And let me do above
What I cannot do here.
If rain and wind and storm in this wilderness
Wear down the tattered garment a little longer,
Then draw the spirit into Your heavenly being,
So that only what is earthly
Remains behind on earth.

597. At the Passing of a Beloved Sister

The sister's joy is truly great;
She receives the final and best portion.
The Shepherd takes the lamb from the heath—
Where to?
To Zion's green pasture.
You others, come—go forward with vigor:
Cheerful walking is followed by blessed rest.
Die to yourselves; live to God from now on,
And your dying will soon be done.
Whoever dies in God
Dies blessed in God—
Though not everyone dies rejoicing.

598. On Divine Illumination in the Ground of the Soul, Unknown to All Worldly Scholars

(After the Latin of Johannes Tauler)

I often understand, in the Ground of the heart,
More than any human being could ever teach me—
Through stillness, from the true Light.
Oh that I might remain Yours when this occurs;
What lofty divine gifts would then be mine!
Yet let it be as God wills.
Therefore sink yourself at every moment
Into the lowest humility
Before God and all creatures.
This alone is true wisdom,
In which all arts are enclosed
And which is necessary for salvation on earth.

599. On Inward Nakedness and Letting Go of Ourselves and All Things

(After Tauler)

I compose a new song of nakedness,
For true purity does not think;
How could there be thoughts
When I have lost what is mine?
I have become undone.

Whoever truly stands inwardly stripped
Is released from every care.
Whether well or ill is all the same to me;
I am as willing to be poor as rich.

THE SPIRITUAL FLOWER GARDEN

I cannot deal with images;
I must stand wholly emptied of myself.
I have become undone.

You ask how I came to freedom from images:
When I perceived true unity within myself
And unity impressed itself so deeply
That neither love nor suffering moved me.
I have become undone.

You ask how I escaped into the Spirit:
When I perceived neither this nor that within myself,
But only bare Godhead without Ground,
I could no longer remain silent—
I had to make it known.
I have become undone.

Since I thus fell into the abyss,
I can no longer speak—I must fall silent;
The clear Godhead
So wholly absorbs me into itself.
I have become undone.

This darkness makes me deeply refreshed and glad
Once I have passed through everything.
At my origin I never grow old;
Like the eagle, I am renewed.
All my powers are truly
Swallowed up and utterly died.

Whoever truly stands inwardly stripped
Is released from every care.

On this dying and becoming undone
The Father, Son, and Spirit
Are revealed to us on earth.
'I am crucified with Christ.' (Gal. 2:20)

All goodness, delight, and pasture—
Far beyond all measure.
But whoever remains un-released
Remains in suffering as punishment.

600. The One Who Composed This Song Felt Thus

(After Tauler)

My spirit
Has wandered and traveled
Into a most sweet
And divinely silent wilderness.
No word
Nor wisdom has any place there;
A Being has embraced me
Where astonishment finds no place.

My spirit
Has wandered and traveled.
Reason and intellect
Do not reach this land;
It lies far beyond all senses.
I will not attempt to seek it.

My spirit
Has wandered and traveled.
Sink yourself only one hour
Into the Ground of your soul;
There uncreated blessedness

Is recognized and offered.
When you fully depart from nothingness,
Then a Nothing is revealed to you—
Unfit for the tongue,
Yet remaining something
For the one who does not seek himself or his own.
Only such a one can grasp it.

601. On a Free Sinking into the Godhead

(After Tauler)

My God has truly comforted me
When I am as empty as I should be;
He restores me and wills to make me new.
If only I could stand entirely free,
Ever going forward with Christ—
That would be the richest thing of all riches.
Yet He wills to bring me still further:
I am to sink into the sea of the Godhead.
There I am without all care;
No voice disturbs me there.
O God, how well, how rich, how blessed
One swims in the sea of the Godhead!
God alone is our concern there;
The heart is full of comfort and joy.
God has promised me this eternal life;
He will surely give it to me—
Only that, freed from the created,
I may be one with the One.
The power of love
Keeps my tender gaze
Ever directed toward God alone.
O God, how well, how rich, how blessed
One swims in the sea of the Godhead!

602. Love of Being Despised

(After Johannes Evangelista)

Gladly to be despised, scorned, set aside;
Gladly to be slandered, hated, finally pursued;
Gladly to be envied for love and beneficence—
This is truly a blessed state before our God.
But where are such wise ones to be found,
That one might rightly praise them?
Nowhere at all, indeed—
This is only too clear.
If such a one exists,
He sits alone and hidden,
Tucked away in a little corner with his little book.
This one I truly call poor in spirit,
Whom Jesus there pronounces blessed.

603. Love Is Strong

(After Gerlach Petersen)

Sweet or bitter, love or suffering
In this valley of misery called time—
What matters it, if only love is pure?
This fire consumes both joy and pain.
Love can endure
Much cross without complaint;
Love sets its hand to the work
And gives strength to resolution.
Love seeks in all things
Only to please God;
Love regards itself as very small
And keeps the heart pure.

604. The Language of Love

(After Jodocus van Lodenstein)

Who can impose such boundaries on one who loves
That love may not freely pour itself into words?
Must love speak according to the thoughts
Of one who has never felt what love is?

605. The Gentle Gaze upon the Crucified

(After Malaval)

This contemplation can bring all thoughts to death;
The heart loses itself in this powerful act.
And when anxieties press heavily upon the poor heart,
The gentle gaze exerts an even stronger pull.

606. Comfort of the Resurrection

(After Prudentius)

No—do not fear, you who are my members:
You shall return to God together with Christ;
Believe this freely!
He bears you as his own,
Calls you with himself from death into life—
He is faithful.
Should sickness threaten, greet it with joy;
Despise distress, affliction, and suffering,
Whatever may come.
Look calmly upon the dark grave;
Go with Christ, the Risen One,
Following him as you are able.

BOOK II
MEDITATIONS AND SPIRITUAL VERSES

BOOK II

PART I: MEDITATIONS FROM THE PROPHETS

Consisting of Concise Meditations on Selected Sayings from the Four Major Prophets, Directed Toward the Inner Life

> *"All Scripture is given by inspiration of God, and is profitable for doctrine, for reproof, for correction, for instruction in righteousness."* 2 Timothy 3:16 (NKJV)

Prefatory Notice

This is precisely the great privilege and distinguishing character of Holy Scripture above all other books in the world: that in everything God has caused to be written therein, something is opened for our benefit, for our instruction, for our correction, and the like.

In some places this lies more plainly and shines almost immediately before every eye; in other places it lies deeper and more hidden, in parables, riddles, and types. Be that as it may: if the saying of the Apostle Paul is to remain true, and if Scripture has not been written for me in vain, then there must nevertheless be something in it for my instruction and for my amendment. And however long I may turn and turn a parable, a history, or any saying spoken or written by Moses or the prophets, by Christ or by His apostles—however finely and correctly I may interpret and apply it to the circumstances and persons to whom it was originally spoken or written—I must at last, willingly or unwillingly, interpret it in reference to my own person. Otherwise I derive no benefit, no instruction, no correction from it; and it would help me toward holiness and salvation no more than if it were not written in the Bible at all.

From this it follows:

1. That it is vain, useless, and even harmful to read and expound Scripture in such a way that one remains only with the letter, the historical matter, and the external circumstances, and spends one's effort in criticizing and disputing about them, without looking into one's own heart to see what is to be found there for one's personal benefit.

2. That it is good and praiseworthy first to understand the external circumstances and the literal sense of a passage in general, but then—and above all—to consider what, in one's own particular circumstances, may serve for instruction and correction.

3. But that the shortest, most fruitful, and best use of Scripture is to apply everything immediately to oneself—each person to his own life, to the state of his soul, and to his circumstances—doing so simply, in the fear of God, and under the guidance of the Spirit of truth.

It is objected that such interpretations of Scripture have no binding authority in themselves. But what blindness is this! Should that which the Holy Spirit Himself impresses upon the heart not bind far more powerfully and convince the soul far more deeply than that which is built upon the loose sand of human reason—where one clever mind is always found that overturns another's arguments and entire system? Or could there be deception or danger in allowing oneself, according to the promise of the Lord Jesus, to be led into all truth by His own Spirit? By no means.

Thus the apostles immediately applied everything inwardly. Without circumlocution or lengthy descriptions of the Passover lamb, circumcision, the temple, and other outward matters, they simply said: "Indeed Christ, our Passover, was sacrificed for us" (1 Corinthians 5:7, NKJV); "We are the circumcision, who worship God in the Spirit" (Philippians 3:3, NKJV); "You are the temple of the living God" (2 Corinthians 6:16, NKJV); and so forth.

Therefore, in order to read and understand Holy Scripture with profit, it is not strictly necessary for a Christian to be experienced in languages, history, textual criticism, and similar human sciences. Rather, from what has been said it is evident that a simple, God-seeking soul is just as capable—indeed far more capable—of this than the most learned and practiced critic. For the critic, by his scholarly conceptions, is continually led away from himself toward others and toward the outer shell, and often spends so much time questioning and researching these things that neither time nor space remains to think of his own edification. Meanwhile, a teachable, inward soul, which goes in and out within itself, without such elaborate preparation, can find its pasture, life, and sufficiency everywhere, without troubling itself about the opinions and arguments of the learned world.

In this sense these few meditations on selected sayings from the prophets have been undertaken. They are so briefly composed that the reader will still have opportunity to ponder much further on his own. No one's private thoughts are to be imposed upon anyone else—still less is any claim made to present the sole meaning of the Spirit in this or that saying; such would be self-will and not the sense of God. "Your commandment is exceedingly broad," says David (Psalm 119:96, NKJV). Whoever, in considering Scripture, has the pure love of God and neighbor as his foundation and aim has grasped the true intention of the Spirit—the intention God had in view when He caused the Bible to be written—and need have no further scruples. For the Lord Jesus Himself says that this is the entire substance of the Law and the Prophets.

To say more on this is not permitted by the narrow limits of space.

May God cause everything to prosper unto blessing.

Meditation 1

> *"If you are willing and obedient, you shall eat the good of the land; but if you refuse and rebel, you shall be devoured by the sword"; for the mouth of the LORD has spoken.* —Isaiah 1:19–20 (NKJV)

God is willing and would give me Himself and every good;
Shall I, a worm, still refuse—shall I long hesitate?
Willingly I leave all behind; willingly I give Him my heart;
Willingly I follow His call, though it bring the flesh its pain.
Speak in the Ground of my soul; draw me there to turn within;
Set me with Mary; speak, Lord—Your servant hears.
Let thought and reason, sense and will, fall silent and be still;
Hew down by Your sword whatever in me would still refuse!

Meditation 2

> *I will turn My hand against you, and thoroughly purge away your dross, and take away all your alloy. I will restore your judges as at the first, and your counselors as at the beginning. Afterward you shall be called the city of righteousness, the faithful city.* —Isaiah 1:25–26 (NKJV)

The lead of false seeming must from us be taken;
The scum of Self-hood must be swept away most purely.
One sees but scum and lead when it comes to the proving,
When God in earnest sets Himself against us as Judge.
Here reason with its counsel helps us little;
Here it is set aside as blind from the judgment-seat.
Wisdom enters into you—becomes Judge, Counselor, and King;
As it was in the beginning, so shall it be at the end.

Meditation 3

> *O house of Jacob, come and let us walk in the light of the LORD.*
> —Isaiah 2:5 (NKJV)

Come, children of Jacob, you who gladly stay at home,
While Esau runs and strives to catch his game!
Yet he still comes up short, however much he labors;
The quiet Jacob is content with blessing alone.
Let us in gentle spirit, detached from all,
Walk ever at home before the Father's face;
Else we remain in night and find no peace—
The Lord's Presence gives life, rest, and light!

Meditation 4

> *The loftiness of man shall be bowed down, and the haughtiness of men shall be made low; the LORD alone will be exalted in that day, but the idols He shall utterly abolish.* —Isaiah 2:17–18 (NKJV)

Lift not yourself, O soul, though you had a thousand gifts,
And were you ever so pious before yourself and all the world;
It comes, it comes—the day when buried shall be in dust
Whatever set itself up so high in you as idol!
Down—bow yourself into Nothingness, you worm of earth;
Cast every idol away; let the Lord alone be high!
Then may God rightly and purely be worshiped in you,
When you are poor in spirit, stripped, and truly small.

Meditation 5

> *When the Lord has washed away the filth of the daughters of Zion, and purged the blood of Jerusalem from her midst, by the spirit of judgment and by the spirit of burning, then the LORD will create above every dwelling place of Mount Zion, and above her assemblies, a cloud and smoke by day and the shining of a flaming fire by night. For over all the glory there will be a covering. And there will be a tabernacle for shade in the daytime from the heat, for a place of refuge, and for a shelter from storm and rain.* —Isaiah 4:4–6 (NKJV)

If Zion's daughter here on earth as bride
Is to be deeply, wholly cleansed from all defilement,
Then sharp the lye must bite; thereafter fire must burn,
Until all dross is parted from the pure gold.
So does the Lord then enter into the sanctuary of souls,
To choose His dwelling there for evermore.
He covers them with the cloud of His secret Presence;
A living fire by night makes all things bright within.
God's glory remains hidden in such humble souls;
For strangers there is shadow, heat, and storm—
But here is found true rest, true shelter, and true shade;
God's faithful Presence shields us and remains.

Meditation 6

> *"Be shattered, O you peoples, and be broken in pieces! Give ear, all you from far countries. Gird yourselves, but be broken in pieces; gird yourselves, but be broken in pieces. Take counsel together, but it will come to nothing; speak the word, but it will not stand, for God is with us." For the LORD spoke thus to me with a strong hand, and instructed me that I should not walk in the way of this people.* —Isaiah 8:9–11 (NKJV)

However the world rages and takes counsel,
And gathers itself mightily against God's kingdom:
It shall be broken; its counsel shall come to nothing;
God is with us—He will preserve His Zion.
So is the soul established which God's hand has grasped,
And which He leads not as the world would go.
Fear not, soul—though all storms rush upon you—
In peace be still; God is with you; He alone is your strength!

Meditation 7

> *And when they say to you, "Seek those who are mediums and wizards, who whisper and mutter," should not a people seek their God? Should they seek the dead on behalf of the living?* —Isaiah 8:19 (NKJV)

Shall not a people seek their God alone,
Who lives and gives life to everything?
Why do you seek what gives no living power,
And gives but whistling wind and empty sound?
Go into your heart; there God will speak to you;
There is the place of oracle—there wait and hear.
Seek not from creatures what they cannot give;
Turn inward—God lives there, the living God!

Meditation 8

> *And in that day you will say: "O LORD, I will praise You; though You were angry with me, Your anger is turned away, and You comfort me. Behold, God is my salvation, I will trust and not be afraid; 'For YAH, the LORD, is my strength and song; He also has become my salvation.'" Therefore with joy you will draw water from the wells of salvation.* —Isaiah 12:1–3 (NKJV)

O that glad day when wrath has turned to grace,
When comfort streams within where fear once dwelt!
The Lord Himself becomes salvation, song, and strength;
In place of dread there comes delight and trust.
O blessed drawing from salvation's wells,
When inwardly the springs of joy break forth!
Here is the soul refreshed in depths of God,
Where living waters flow that never fail.

Meditation 9

> *In that day a man will look to his Maker, and his eyes will have respect for the Holy One of Israel. He will not look to the altars, the work of his hands; he will not respect what his fingers have made, nor the wooden images nor the incense altars.* —Isaiah 17:7–8 (NKJV)

When God begins His work to draw the soul,
The eye turns from the creature to the Maker.
The idols that one's fingers fashioned fall—
Those altars built by self and reason's labor.
O happy soul that looks to God alone,
And lets all creature-works lie in the dust!
The Holy One of Israel is your God;
On Him alone set now your heart's regard.

Meditation 10

> *You will keep him in perfect peace, whose mind is stayed on You, because he trusts in You. Trust in the LORD forever, for in YAH, the LORD, is everlasting strength.* —Isaiah 26:3–4 (NKJV)

O blessed peace that nothing can destroy,
When heart and mind are stayed on God alone!
Here thought finds rest; here is the spirit still;
Here trust takes root in the Eternal Rock.
Trust in the Lord—for in Him is your strength;
Let nothing move you from this quiet Ground.
Yah is the Lord—the everlasting Rock;
In Him alone is peace that has no end.

Meditation 11

> *Yes, in the way of Your judgments, O LORD, we have waited for You; the desire of our soul is for Your name and for the remembrance of You. With my soul I have desired You in the night, yes, by my spirit within me I will seek You early; for when Your judgments are in the earth, the inhabitants of the world will learn righteousness.* —Isaiah 26:8–9 (NKJV)

The way of God is through His judgments deep;
Here must the soul learn patience, waiting still.
My one desire, O Lord, is for Your name—
To keep remembrance of You in my heart.
My soul has longed for You through darkest night;
My spirit rises early, seeking You.
When judgment visits earth, then souls awake;
Through trial alone the world learns righteousness.

Meditation 12

> *LORD, You will establish peace for us, for You have also done all our works in us. O LORD our God, masters besides You have had dominion over us; but by You only we make mention of Your name.* —Isaiah 26:12–13 (NKJV)

All that is done in us, the Lord has done;
He works the work; He gives the peace within.
How many lords have ruled us in our blindness—
Self-will, and reason, creatures without end!
Now, Lord, by You alone we call on You;
No other name do we confess but Yours.
Take full dominion—rule alone within;
Establish peace that none but You can give.

Meditation 13

> *Come, my people, enter your chambers, and shut your doors behind you; hide yourself, as it were, for a little moment, until the indignation is past.* —Isaiah 26:20 (NKJV)

Come, soul, into your chamber—enter in;
Shut fast the door against all outward things.
Hide yourself here in stillness, out of sight,
Until the storms of judgment pass away.
A little moment seems so hard to bear,
Yet soon it ends, and God Himself appears.
Be hidden, soul—the safest place is here,
Deep in the Ground, in God, in quiet rest.

Meditation 14

> "I, the LORD, keep it, I water it every moment; lest any hurt it, I keep it night and day. Fury is not in Me. Who would set briers and thorns against Me in battle? I would go through them, I would burn them together." —Isaiah 27:3–4 (NKJV)

Who is a vineyard of God stands eternally well-kept;
Not a good work nor word, not a single leaf is lost.
God guards him day and night, in joy and in pain,
And pours into him His sap of life each moment.
God is to such a one Love only—in Him is no wrath to be found;
Sin, reason, and Self-hood must alone the wrath endure.
Such hedges He tears down; such thorns must be consumed,
Ere God can freely flow into our Ground as Love.

Meditation 15

> "Whom will he teach knowledge? And whom will he make to understand the message? Those just weaned from milk? Those just drawn from the breasts?" —Isaiah 28:9 (NKJV)

From honor, gold, and earthly pleasure
Must heart and sense be weaned away;
Yea, to the sweetness of the spirit
Cling nevermore in Self-hood's way.
Leave such a breast; remain detached,
Nailed to the cross, content with God!
Who thus in spirit hears God Himself
Becomes most learned without study.

Meditation 16

> *For thus says the Lord GOD, the Holy One of Israel: "In returning and rest you shall be saved; in quietness and confidence shall be your strength." But you would not."*—Isaiah 30:15 (NKJV)

Ah, one runs here and there, thinking thus to find the treasure—
Soul, your pain remains where you will not still be.
Break your own will; let creatures disappear;
Turn inward and wait there—
So is God's help at hand!
Reason's busyness and the flightiness of the senses,
All multiplicity—bring gently into unity.
Remain thus trustingly still; God is near within you;
Stillness and good courage
Do great deeds with God!

Meditation 17

> *And though the Lord gives you the bread of adversity and the water of affliction, yet your teachers will not be moved into a corner anymore, but your eyes shall see your teachers. Your ears shall hear a word behind you, saying, "This is the way, walk in it," whenever you turn to the right hand or whenever you turn to the left.* —Isaiah 30:20–21 (NKJV)

One must not remain standing with teachers outside oneself;
That which can awaken us comes and goes away.
O blessed, who within himself can see God with his eyes—
He has the Teacher near, upon whom all depends!
He hears the eternal Word speak in the still Ground:
"So turn yourself, My child, from all things into Me;
This is the way alone—you need not always ask;
Go only straight ahead; mark what I teach you!"

Meditation 18

> *Like birds flying about, so will the LORD of hosts defend Jerusalem. Defending, He will also deliver it; passing over, He will preserve it. Return to Him against whom the children of Israel have deeply revolted.* —Isaiah 31:5–6 (NKJV)

Hear how lovingly the Lord will cover His Jerusalem,
As the birds' wings stretch themselves over their young!
Wayward children, hear—turn back and turn within,
If with Jerusalem you would be so preserved!
Lord, You call; I am coming—let my heart here on earth
Become Your dear City of Peace and thus be guarded.
Rescue me from the enemy's power; come dwell within my heart;
Walk in me day and night, as in Your own possession!

Meditation 19

> *But a generous man devises generous things, and by generosity he shall stand.* —Isaiah 32:8 (NKJV)

A prince and lord of the world I should have been in Adam,
Yet now a slave am I, from Adam's line born.
Into the first nobility Christ leads me back again;
He has chosen me as His bride and queen.
Away then, creature—you are far too base for me!
My spirit, heart, and mind shall rise in God alone.
With great things only does a prince transact his business—
Should I not live befitting my station before God's eyes!

Meditation 20

> *He who walks righteously and speaks uprightly, he who despises the gain of oppressions, who gestures with his hands, refusing bribes, who stops his ears from hearing of bloodshed, and shuts his eyes from seeing evil: he will dwell on high; his place of defense will be the fortress of rocks; bread will be given him, his water will be sure. Your eyes will see the King in His beauty; they will see the land that is very far off.* —Isaiah 33:15–17 (NKJV)

Who shuts his eyes, nothing vain to see,
And, loosed and stripped from all, turns inward into God,
Can like an eagle ever stand exalted in the spirit
And remain untouched by unrest, fear, and pain.
In this high fortress, far above all senses,
In the Rock Jesus alone he builds his dwelling;
He finds bread of life and water enough therein—
His eye beholds the King there in His beauty.

Meditation 21

> *Strengthen the weak hands, and make firm the feeble knees. Say to those who are fearful-hearted, "Be strong, do not fear! Behold, your God will come with vengeance, with the recompense of God; He will come and save you."* —Isaiah 35:3–4 (NKJV)

Wavering heart, yield not; strengthen your weary hands;
Walk on and sink not utterly down in your misery.
Yea, fainthearted one, take courage; fear not and stand firm;
Trust God—He is so faithful that He never forsakes the weak!

Soon comes the joyful day when God shall enter into you;
Then will you thank Him still, when you shall hear Him for yourself;
Then will you see Him near, who now seems so far away.
Only watch and look—God shall destroy your enemies!

Meditation 22

> *And the remnant who have escaped of the house of Judah shall again take root downward, and bear fruit upward. For out of Jerusalem shall go a remnant, and those who escape from Mount Zion. The zeal of the LORD of hosts will do this.* —Isaiah 37:31–32 (NKJV)

God's remnant takes root deep in the Ground below,
And upward into God brings forth the fruit of life.
The outward things must perish—only Zion shall remain;
What is of God escapes and lives eternally.
Lord, let me be among the remnant that You save,
Deep-rooted, fruit-bearing, wholly Yours within!
Your zeal shall do it—not my strength or will;
I sink into Your working, and Your work is done.

Meditation 23

> *The voice said, "Cry out!" And he said, "What shall I cry?" "All flesh is grass, and all its loveliness is like the flower of the field. The grass withers, the flower fades, because the breath of the LORD blows upon it; surely the people are grass. The grass withers, the flower fades, but the word of our God stands forever."* —Isaiah 40:6–8 (NKJV)

What is all flesh? A flower that fades away;
A grass that withers when God's breath comes near.
The fairest beauty passes like a dream;
What seemed so lovely crumbles into dust.

But God's word stands forever, firm and true—
One thing alone endures when all things fail.
O soul, build not on grass that withers fast;
Take root in God, whose word can never pass.

Meditation 24

But those who wait on the LORD shall renew their strength; they shall mount up with wings like eagles, they shall run and not be weary, they shall walk and not faint. —Isaiah 40:31 (NKJV)

Who waits upon the Lord renews his strength within;
He rises up on wings, as eagles soar on high.
He runs and does not weary; walks and does not faint;
The Lord Himself becomes his power and his life.
O blessed waiting—still before the Lord—
Here is the secret of the soul's true strength!
Not striving, running, laboring in self,
But resting, trusting, waiting upon God.

Meditation 25

"The poor and needy seek water, but there is none, their tongues fail for thirst. I, the LORD, will hear them; I, the God of Israel, will not forsake them. I will open rivers in desolate heights, and fountains in the midst of the valleys; I will make the wilderness a pool of water, and the dry land springs of water." —Isaiah 41:17-18 (NKJV)

Poor soul, who thirsts and finds no water near,
Whose tongue is parched within a barren land—
The Lord has heard you; He will not forsake;
His hand shall open rivers in the waste.
Where all was dry, there springs shall break forth now;

The wilderness shall bloom with pools of life.
Wait, thirsty one—God's streams are flowing near;
He makes the desert blossom for His own.

Meditation 26

> *"Behold! My Servant whom I uphold, My Elect One in whom My soul delights! I have put My Spirit upon Him; He will bring forth justice to the Gentiles. He will not cry out, nor raise His voice, nor cause His voice to be heard in the street. A bruised reed He will not break, and smoking flax He will not quench; He will bring forth justice for truth. He will not fail nor be discouraged, till He has established justice in the earth; and the coastlands shall wait for His law."* —Isaiah 42:1–4 (NKJV)

Behold the Servant whom the Father loves,
In whom His soul delights—the chosen One!
His Spirit rests upon Him, full and true;
He works in stillness, not with noise and show.
The bruised reed He handles with such care;
The smoking wick He tends and will not quench.
With patient love He labors for the truth,
Until His justice fills the waiting earth.

Meditation 27

> *But now, thus says the LORD, who created you, O Jacob, and He who formed you, O Israel: "Fear not, for I have redeemed you; I have called you by your name; you are Mine. When you pass through the waters, I will be with you; and through the rivers, they shall not overflow you. When you walk through the fire, you shall not be burned, nor shall the flame scorch you."* —Isaiah 43:1–2 (NKJV)

Fear not, O soul—the Lord who made you speaks:
"I have redeemed you; you are Mine alone.
I call you by your name—you belong to Me;
Through water, fire, and flood I hold you fast."
Though rivers rise, they shall not overflow;
Though flames leap high, they shall not burn your soul.
Your God is with you—He who formed your being;
In every trial His presence is your shield.

Meditation 28

> *"Do not remember the former things, nor consider the things of old. Behold, I will do a new thing, now it shall spring forth; shall you not know it? I will even make a road in the wilderness and rivers in the desert. The beast of the field will honor Me, the jackals and the ostriches, because I give waters in the wilderness and rivers in the desert, to give drink to My people, My chosen. This people I have formed for Myself; they shall declare My praise."* —Isaiah 43:18–21 (NKJV)

Forget what lies behind—the old has passed;
Behold, the Lord is doing something new!
A road springs forth where none had ever been;
Rivers break out across the desert sand.
This new creation honors God alone;
His chosen people drink His living streams.
He formed them for Himself—they are His own;
Their only purpose: to declare His praise.

Meditation 29

> *"I, even I, am He who blots out your transgressions for My own sake; and I will not remember your sins."* —Isaiah 43:25 (NKJV)

God blots out all transgression for His sake—
Not for your merit, but because He wills.
Your sins He casts behind Him, clean away;
He will not bring them back to memory.
O grace that needs no earning, no repay!
God acts for His name's sake, not yours alone.
Rest here, poor sinner—all your guilt is gone;
The Lord Himself has wiped the record clean.

Meditation 30

> *"Remember these, O Jacob, and Israel, for you are My servant; I have formed you, you are My servant; O Israel, you will not be forgotten by Me! I have blotted out, like a thick cloud, your transgressions, and like a cloud, your sins. Return to Me, for I have redeemed you."* —Isaiah 44:21-22 (NKJV)

Remember, soul—you are God's servant still;
He formed you, made you, calls you by His name.
You shall not be forgotten or cast off;
His love holds fast through all your wandering ways.
Like clouds that vanish in the morning light,
Your sins are blotted out and gone forever.
Return, return—for He has paid the price;
Come home to Him who has redeemed your soul.

Meditation 31

> *"Fear not, for I am with you; I will bring your descendants from the east, and gather you from the west."* —Isaiah 43:5 (NKJV)

This is the cause, poor soul, that you hover in fear:
That God is not with you and you live not with God.
When this Essence draws near and one becomes united with Him,
Then must the feeblest heart be comforted and still.
This is so indeed, my God—yet often am I in care
Whether You are with me when You have hidden Yourself from me.
Therefore I, poor one, ever fear so in dark ways.
Help me believe that You are near—so shall I be still and glad!

Meditation 32

> *"I, even I, am the LORD, and besides Me there is no savior."* —Isaiah 43:11 (NKJV)

I am, I am, whatever you can ever desire;
I am, I am—and not the creature.
The creature lasts not long; it cannot nourish the spirit;
Your God, your Good am I, Jehovah, only.
I alone can heal your sin's misery;
Your own doing, O soul, suffices not.
Turn inward into Me; if you will not divide your heart,
Then I give you here already blessedness and rest!

Meditation 33

> *"Yes, you have burdened Me with your sins, you have wearied Me with your iniquities. I, even I, am He who blots out your transgressions for My own sake; and I will not remember your sins."* —Isaiah 43:24–25 (NKJV)

Yes, labor did You have, O Jesus, from my sins;
You had to bear their load in body and in soul.
You are, You are the only One who has redeemed me;
Yet still I make You toil through my misdeed.
Ah, blot out my sin completely from my heart—
To You it causes toil, to me such bitter pain—
For Your own sake alone, because You are Jesus,
That I may love and honor You as is Your desire!

Meditation 34

> *"That they may know from the rising of the sun to its setting that there is none besides Me. I am the LORD, and there is no other; I form the light and create darkness, I make peace and create calamity; I, the LORD, do all these things."* — Isaiah 45:6–7 (NKJV)

Give heart and will entirely; let God as Lord hold sway therein.
One must not counsel with—no, God is Lord alone!
World, you do lose your claim, and those who side with you.
My Lord, only command—I will be Your slave!
Ah, let me live immovably dependent upon You
And receive both light and darkness from You only!
You do permit the evil; You will give the peace;
Therefore my faith speaks ever: The Lord—He has done it.

Meditation 35

> *"Truly You are God, who hide Yourself, O God of Israel, the Savior!"* —Isaiah 45:15 (NKJV)

O hidden God, in whom we all do live,
When will You become manifest to me in the spirit?
My searching reason must give itself captive;
In the dark Ground, simplicity becomes aware of You.

Who can, O hidden God, fathom the wondrous ways
By which, my Savior, You sanctify Your own?
Your people are hidden—who can find himself therein,
That poverty, cross, and shame are Your children's ornament?

Meditation 36

> *"Look to Me, and be saved, all you ends of the earth! For I am God, and there is no other. I have sworn by Myself; the word has gone out of My mouth in righteousness, and shall not return, that to Me every knee shall bow, every tongue shall take an oath. He shall say, 'Surely in the LORD I have righteousness and strength.'"* —Isaiah 45:22–24 (NKJV)

Blessedness, O soul, is easy to obtain:
You need only turn your heart and love
Wholly from yourself and every creature
Unto God alone—so shall He satisfy you.
Let Him be your God, your Good, and none else;
Bow your knee, adore, give Him the honor;
Forget yourself; look not upon your own works—
In God alone is righteousness and strength!

Meditation 37

> *"Listen to Me, O house of Jacob, and all the remnant of the house of Israel, who have been upheld by Me from birth, who have been carried from the womb: Even to your old age, I am He, and even to gray hairs I will carry you! I have made, and I will bear; even I will carry, and will deliver you. To whom will you liken Me, and make Me equal, and compare Me, that we may be like?"* —Isaiah 46:3–5 (NKJV)

How high, how deep, how broad is our God's goodness!
O sea of kindness—what shall I say?
You lift me and carry me in body and in inmost heart;
You have long done it and do it still.
A mother loves her child whom she has carried in her womb;
You, more than mother's heart, carry me evermore.
Though I lie in misery, yet I hear You say:
"I will deliver you." To whom should I compare You?

Meditation 38

> *"Remember this, and show yourselves men; recall to mind, O you transgressors."* —Isaiah 46:8 (NKJV)

You transgressors, go into your heart within—
So will the godly God teach the sinner repentance!
He shall in faith turn inward from all things
With heart and desire and mind, and love God alone.
In the heart, God and all things become manifest to us.
I, a transgressor, am yet so distracted and far off;
Draw me in, my God—I would so gladly
Turn into my heart and into Your heart altogether!

Meditation 39

> *"Thus says the LORD, your Redeemer, the Holy One of Israel: 'I am the LORD your God, who teaches you to profit, who leads you by the way you should go.'"* —Isaiah 48:17 (NKJV)

A master, soul, you do need for learning—
God Himself is such and also wishes to be so.
His teaching is not empty; His word can nourish the spirit;
His leading leads straight into the true life.
Soul, mark what God teaches you; remain still and detached,

And follow, as a child, the faithful guidance only.
So shall a gentle stream bring you deep peace,
And your godliness shall be mighty and great.

Meditation 40

> "Oh, that you had heeded My commandments! Then your peace would have been like a river, and your righteousness like the waves of the sea." —Isaiah 48:18 (NKJV)

O, if one would but gladly learn obedience
And follow God in all with willing trust!
Then would the blessed life so sweetly flow
Like streams of peace and waves of righteousness.
Ah Lord, I am so stubborn, so unwilling still;
I choose my own way and thus lose Your peace.
Break my will; give me a yielded heart,
That Your commandments may become my delight!

Meditation 41

> "Listen, O coastlands, to Me, and take heed, you peoples from afar! The LORD has called Me from the womb; from the matrix of My mother He has made mention of My name." —Isaiah 49:1 (NKJV)

Hear it, O nations far and near—hear God's beloved Son!
He speaks for your salvation; attend to what He says.
From His mother's womb the Father has called Him;
His name was known before the world began.
O Jesus, let me also hear Your voice within;
Speak to my heart and call me by my name.
You have known me before I was—now let me know You,
That I may love and follow You alone!

Meditation 42

> *"But Zion said, 'The LORD has forsaken me, and my Lord has forgotten me.' Can a woman forget her nursing child, and not have compassion on the son of her womb? Surely they may forget, yet I will not forget you. See, I have inscribed you on the palms of My hands; your walls are continually before Me."* —Isaiah 49:14–16 (NKJV)

Many think they stand well when God's grace refreshes them;
Many who are in suffering
Think that God forgets them.
Parched Zion, be content with what God takes and what He sends;
You must learn to love purely—
Not the gifts, but God alone!
He—God Himself—forsakes you not;
He can never forget you;
Your soul in His hand
Is far too well known to Him.
Children of the cross His heart loves with mercy beyond measure;
Only think on God alone—
He will not forget you!

Meditation 43

> *"He is near who justifies Me; who will contend with Me? Let us stand together. Who is My adversary? Let him come near to Me. Surely the Lord GOD will help Me; who is he who will condemn Me? Indeed they will all grow old like a garment; the moth will eat them up."* —Isaiah 50:8–9 (NKJV)

O blessed, who is wedded to God in chaste love,
Who is wholly the Lord's, whom He rules as He wills!
Then let who will contend—no foe disturbs or torments him;
He who speaks for him is near; the Lord defends him.

Who then has a claim on me? I belong to the Lord;
My heart belongs to Him alone and to no other.
God helps—only try, you shall not bend me!
God helps—only condemn, I remain still at rest!

Meditation 44

> *"Who among you fears the LORD? Who obeys the voice of His Servant? Who walks in darkness and has no light? Let him trust in the name of the LORD and rely upon his God."* —Isaiah 50:10 (NKJV)

Who fears the Lord alone, who gladly follows His voice
And must walk in darkness—think not: the Lord is far!
Though the sun shine not for you, yet the sun is there;
After darkness comes light; if you seek God, He is near.
Grow not dismayed in the dark; hope in the Lord's name;
Think: Jehovah is faithful; what He speaks is Yea and Amen.
Lean upon your God; hold Him fast, so you shall not fall.
Believe: you go surer thus than in your own light!

Meditation 45

> *"So the ransomed of the LORD shall return, and come to Zion with singing, with everlasting joy on their heads. They shall obtain joy and gladness; sorrow and sighing shall flee away."* —Isaiah 51:11 (NKJV)

Wait only, burdened soul, you who are captive within yourself,
Whose spirit cannot attain to freedom as it would.
Hear—your Redeemer comes; after many thousand "Ah" and "O"
You shall at last be redeemed; you shall at last be glad!

Then shall your lively spirit freely turn into its Origin
And with rejoicing honor your God in Himself in Zion.
Sweet bliss crowns your head—joy and life without end;
All sighing flees away from the still Element.

Meditation 46

> *"How beautiful upon the mountains are the feet of him who brings good news, who proclaims peace, who brings glad tidings of good things, who proclaims salvation, who says to Zion, 'Your God reigns!' Your watchmen shall lift up their voices, with their voices they shall sing together; for they shall see eye to eye when the LORD brings back Zion."* —Isaiah 52:7–8 (NKJV)

Yes, how lovely is it when the soul, after long lamenting,
Hears this message within from the Savior Himself:
Your God is King in you; your burdened heart is free
From the bondage of Selfhood, from the slavery of sins.
Peace, peace be with you; all good, salvation, and life
Is freely proclaimed and given to you in the one Good.
Your eyes see it now—that your sighing is heard!
That is truly to be converted, when the Lord Himself converts us.

Meditation 47

> *"Depart! Depart! Go out from there, touch no unclean thing; go out from the midst of her, be clean, you who bear the vessels of the LORD. For you shall not go out with haste, nor go by flight; for the LORD will go before you, and the God of Israel will be your rear guard."* —Isaiah 52:11–12 (NKJV)

If the Highest would choose you for priestly service unto Him,
To stand before Him in the spirit with offering and prayer:
Depart, depart into solitude;
Depart, depart into the Ground of the soul;
Your heart and sense must wholly go out from all that is vain.
Yes, let no thought touch what is unclean;
Go out from Selfhood; be without blemish, pure.
See, God goes before and follows; let yourself be simply led;
Run not forward in flight—you must be circumspect!

Meditation 48

> *"For He shall grow up before Him as a tender plant, and as a root out of dry ground. He has no form or comeliness; and when we see Him, there is no beauty that we should desire Him. He is despised and rejected by men, a Man of sorrows and acquainted with grief. And we hid, as it were, our faces from Him; He was despised, and we did not esteem Him."*
> —Isaiah 53:2–3 (NKJV)

Behold, how Jesus grows up—how hidden, how lowly!
One sees therein no beauty that pleases the natural eye.
He who would see the beauty there
Must also go down with Him.
Who gets a little light and grace would unawares rise like Adam.
My God, how deep must one then bow to the grave in that wilderness,
Bereft of life and comfort and light,
Until one has become utterly nothing!
There first becomes the land of the living
And its beauty known in the Ground.

Meditation 49

> *"Surely He has borne our griefs and carried our sorrows; yet we esteemed Him stricken, smitten by God, and afflicted. But He was wounded for our transgressions, He was bruised for our iniquities; the chastisement for our peace was upon Him, and by His stripes we are healed."* —Isaiah 53:4–5 (NKJV)

O my Jesus, what great loads You carry for me!
My sickness and my sorrow lie upon Your heart.
We thought You were smitten by God,
But it was our burden that pressed You down.
For my sins You were wounded, for my guilt You were crushed;
The punishment that brings me peace fell upon You.
Through Your stripes I am healed—what grace, what love!
Let me live for You alone, who died for me!

Meditation 50

> *"All we like sheep have gone astray; we have turned, every one, to his own way; and the LORD has laid on Him the iniquity of us all."* —Isaiah 53:6 (NKJV)

We all like sheep had gone astray,
Each one to his own way had turned;
But God laid upon Him, the Innocent One,
The sins of us all.
O my soul, see your Shepherd, how He suffers for you!
Stray no more; return to His fold.
He has borne your wandering; He has paid your debt;
Now live only for Him who gave His life for you!

Meditation 51

> *"He was oppressed and He was afflicted, yet He opened not His mouth; He was led as a lamb to the slaughter, and as a sheep before its shearers is silent, so He opened not His mouth."* —Isaiah 53:7 (NKJV)

See how the Lamb is led—so still, so yielded!
He opens not His mouth; He makes no complaint.
Before His shearers silent, before His slaughterers still—
O blessed yieldedness, teach me this silence!
When suffering comes, when enemies press,
Let me learn from You to be still and not resist.
A yielded lamb knows no self-defense;
Make me such a lamb, led only by Your hand!

Meditation 52

> *"And they made His grave with the wicked—but with the rich at His death, because He had done no violence, nor was any deceit in His mouth."* —Isaiah 53:9 (NKJV)

Among the wicked they assigned His grave,
Though no deceit was found in His mouth.
O pure and innocent Lamb, what shame You bore for me!
You died as a sinner, though sin You never knew.
Grant me such innocence, such purity of heart,
That no deceit be found upon my lips.
If I must suffer shame undeserved,
Let me bear it silently with You, my Lord!

Meditation 53

> *"Yet it pleased the LORD to bruise Him; He has put Him to grief. When You make His soul an offering for sin, He shall see His seed, He shall prolong His days, and the pleasure of the LORD shall prosper in His hand."* —Isaiah 53:10 (NKJV)

The Father's will—that Jesus should be crushed—
What mystery of love lies hidden here!
His soul an offering—and yet He lives;
His days prolonged, His seed multiplied.
The Father's pleasure prospers in His hand—
Through death comes life, through suffering comes glory.
Let me too be crushed beneath Your will,
That Your pleasure may prosper in me!

Meditation 54

> *"I will declare your righteousness and your works, for they will not profit you. When you cry out, let your collection of idols deliver you. But the wind will carry them all away, a breath will take them. But he who puts his trust in Me shall possess the land, and shall inherit My holy mountain. And one shall say, 'Heap it up! Heap it up! Prepare the way, take the stumbling block out of the way of My people.'"* —Isaiah 57:12–14 (NKJV)

One's own works profit nothing;
If you would inherit Canaan's rest,
Learn to die to your own doing through yielded suffering.
So stripped, flee then with trust into God,
Until the sweet land of peace—God's holy mountain—is yours!
Fair mountain of holiness, where the eye sees only God;

Still land of eternity, where the peace of God blooms;
Where the long-burdened spirit finds room and open way
And in the Immeasurable can live without stumbling!

Meditation 55

> *"For thus says the High and Lofty One who inhabits eternity, whose name is Holy: 'I dwell in the high and holy place, with him who has a contrite and humble spirit, to revive the spirit of the humble, and to revive the heart of the contrite ones.'"* —Isaiah 57:15 (NKJV)

O high Majesty, who dwells exalted
In still eternity, in the dark sanctuary—
I pray that You, O Holiness, will spare me
According to Your kindness, as I come to You.
Ah, make my spirit humble, gentle, and small,
And dwell then also in me, since You have delight therein!
Here I lie as though dead; Your countenance alone
And Your Spirit's power can make me live.

Meditation 56

> *"If you turn away your foot from the Sabbath, from doing your pleasure on My holy day, and call the Sabbath a delight, the holy day of the LORD honorable, and shall honor Him, not doing your own ways, nor finding your own pleasure, nor speaking your own words, then you shall delight yourself in the LORD; and I will cause you to ride on the high hills of the earth."* —Isaiah 58:13–14 (NKJV)

Worship in self-will, doing good with constraint and complaint,
Keeping Sabbath with vexation—this cannot please the Lord.
Do and speak never what you will and what pleases you;
This is Sabbath: when one holds oneself inwardly yielded to God!

Let this be your heart's delight: so to honor God's Sabbath
And to turn inward into the still sanctuary of your spirit.
Then shall God also be your delight, who lifts you above all,
So that your spirit, content and still, ever lives in Sabbath-rest.

Meditation 57

> *"But your iniquities have separated you from your God; and your sins have hidden His face from you, so that He will not hear."* —Isaiah 59:2 (NKJV)

Your sins, O soul, have made a wall between
You and your God—they hide His face from you.
You cry, but He will not hear; you seek, but cannot find;
The darkness of iniquity has blocked the Light.
Away, away with all that separates!
Let nothing stand between you and your God.
Confess, forsake, be cleansed—then draw near;
His face shall shine on you, and He shall hear!

Meditation 58

> *"So shall they fear the name of the LORD from the west, and His glory from the rising of the sun; when the enemy comes in like a flood, the Spirit of the LORD will lift up a standard against him."* —Isaiah 59:19 (NKJV)

When the enemy floods in—when sorrows overwhelm—
Then the Spirit of the Lord lifts up His standard.
Fear not the rising tide; God's power is greater still;
His name is feared from west to east.
O soul, when floods assail you, stand and see
The Lord's own banner raised against your foe.
He fights for you who cannot fight yourself;
His glory shall arise where darkness seemed to rule!

Meditation 59

> *"Arise, shine; for your light has come! And the glory of the LORD is risen upon you."* —Isaiah 60:1 (NKJV)

Arise, arise, O soul—your light has come!
The glory of the Lord is risen upon you.
Though darkness covers the earth and peoples dwell in night,
Upon you the Lord arises, and His glory appears.
Shine then, O soul, with borrowed light—
Not your own glory, but His who fills you.
Let the nations see His light in you;
Arise and shine—your morning has begun!

Meditation 60

> *"The sun shall no longer be your light by day, nor for brightness shall the moon give light to you; but the LORD will be to you an everlasting light, and your God your glory."* —Isaiah 60:19 (NKJV)

No more shall sun or moon be needed then—
The Lord Himself shall be your everlasting light.
All creature-light shall fade before His glory;
Your God shall be your glory evermore.
O blessed state, when nothing shines between
Your soul and God—when He alone is seen!
Your days of mourning then shall end;
The Lord, your everlasting Light, shall never set!

Meditation 61

Moreover the word of the LORD came to me, saying, "Go and cry in the hearing of Jerusalem, saying, 'Thus says the LORD: I remember you, the kindness of your youth, the love of your betrothal, when you went after Me in the wilderness, in a land not sown. Israel was holiness to the LORD, the firstfruits of His increase. All that devour him will offend; disaster will come upon them,' says the LORD." —Jeremiah 2:1–3 (NKJV)

The Highest Himself here praises the faithfulness of first love,
When the soul vowed herself to Him forever as His bride.
How chaste and tender was the heart; how willing was the mind!
She left the world and followed God with confidence into the wilderness—
The wilderness, where for God's sake she would forgo the creature;
The wilderness, where she would know nothing else but Jesus Christ.
There was the soul so fair and devout;
There was she God's sanctuary.
To whom God has given this grace,
Let him hold fast the crown he has!

Meditation 62

Your own wickedness will correct you, and your backslidings will rebuke you. Know therefore and see that it is an evil and bitter thing that you have forsaken the LORD your God, and the fear of Me is not in you," says the Lord GOD of hosts. —Jeremiah 2:19 (NKJV)

All my evil springs from this alone:
That I forsake You, O Fount of all goodness.
Ah, what bitterness it brings my soul
When I set not Your fear always before my eyes!
This have I long known; now I see what comes of it—
How You forsake him who first forsook You.
Lord, hold me near to You, that I may live in reverence
Before Your eyes always; only this is good and sweet!

Meditation 63

> *"They say, 'If a man divorces his wife, and she goes from him and becomes another man's, may he return to her again?' Would not that land be greatly polluted? But you have played the harlot with many lovers; yet return to Me," says the LORD.* —Jeremiah 3:1 (NKJV)

I myself am that wicked wife who forsook her husband;
I went astray from God, wandering on foreign paths.
I ran after many base lovers; I made myself common;
My heart went into the creature, and it into my heart.
O Abyss of all love and faithfulness, You call me back still!
I sink down before Your feet in shame and thankfulness.
Nothing shall henceforth part me from You; the covenant shall be eternal.
You are my true and rightful Husband, my Lord and God alone.

Meditation 64

> *"Go and proclaim these words toward the north, and say: 'Return, backsliding Israel,' says the LORD; 'I will not cause My anger to fall on you. For I am merciful,' says the LORD; 'I will not remain angry forever. Only acknowledge your iniquity, that you have transgressed against the LORD your God, and have scattered your charms to alien deities*

> *under every green tree, and you have not obeyed My voice,'
> says the LORD. 'Return, O backsliding children,' says the
> LORD; 'for I am married to you. I will take you, one from
> a city and two from a family, and I will bring you to
> Zion.'"* —Jeremiah 3:12–14 (NKJV)

Come, turn inward again, O outward-turned soul,
And remain no longer far off in the land of midnight.
Come, and do not torment yourself with fear and unbelief;
God calls and waits already until you are set aright!
Only confess your guilt and bow yourself humbly;
Turn trustingly thus into His bosom.
Ah no, He is not angry; He is so gracious and kind;
With poor children the Lord would be trusted!

Meditation 65

> *"But I said: 'How can I put you among the children and give
> you a pleasant land, a beautiful heritage of the hosts of
> nations?' And I said: 'You shall call Me, "My Father," and
> not turn away from Me.'"* —Jeremiah 3:19 (NKJV)

You have promised me; when then shall it come to pass,
That the Spirit of adoption sets me among Your children?
I must still stand afar off with fear, as a servant.
Make me free toward You; deliver me at last!
Ah, the longed-for land will You finally give me;
Open soon in me the land of eternity.
Take possession of my inmost; let no heathen live therein;
Then I shall call You "Abba" and depart not from You!

Meditation 66

> *O Jerusalem, wash your heart from wickedness, that you may be saved. How long shall your evil thoughts lodge within you?*
> —Jeremiah 4:14 (NKJV)

God gladly helps all, yet you must be upright;
If you have a false heart, your faith is worthless.
Dissemble not; God knows your Ground;
Even your thoughts, O soul, are known to Him!
Thoughts not from God and that lead not to God
You must lose as vanity, wherever you find them.
Lord, help me ever watch; many storm upon me—
Yet into my lodging shall nothing enter but You!

Meditation 67

> *Thus says the LORD: "Stand in the ways and see, and ask for the old paths, where the good way is, and walk in it; then you will find rest for your souls. But they said, 'We will not walk in it.'"* —Jeremiah 6:16 (NKJV)

How good is the old way—the inward Christian life—
To which the patriarchs gave themselves from the beginning!
They knew no show nor strife of opinions; they died to the creature;
They lived ever in communion with God through faith and love alone.
This is called the secret teaching in these dark days;
Men fear this good way; they will not ask after it.
Blessed is he who has seen this way—let him close his eyes
And walk confidently therein to true soul-rest!

Meditation 68

> *"For I did not speak to your fathers, or command them in the day that I brought them out of the land of Egypt, concerning burnt offerings or sacrifices. But this is what I commanded them, saying, 'Obey My voice, and I will be your God, and you shall be My people. And walk in all the ways that I have commanded you, that it may be well with you.'"* — Jeremiah 7:22–23 (NKJV)

No show nor sacrificial service helps; God seeks not outward works.
Turn inward and there attend inwardly only to God's voice!
You hear it when all is still—reason and self-will too.
Only yield yourself wholly in obedience to God's leading.
In all ways follow only, even when you can see nothing;
Believe it: who remains yielded to God, it cannot go ill with him!
He leads His people and possession into Canaan's rest;
There shall the Lord be your God and Good, and all that you desire.

Meditation 69

> *Thus says the LORD: "Let not the wise man glory in his wisdom, let not the mighty man glory in his might, nor let the rich man glory in his riches; but let him who glories glory in this, that he understands and knows Me, that I am the LORD, exercising lovingkindness, judgment, and righteousness in the earth. For in these I delight," says the LORD.*
> —Jeremiah 9:23–24 (NKJV)

Seek not to have much wisdom and power, nor money and goods;
Boast not even in the inward light of gifted strength and graces!
It is all the Lord's indeed, yet He Himself is not these things;
Therefore remain content with God alone, when all else fails.
How fair and pure is the mind that builds on God alone,

Who looks not upon what he is and can and has as his own,
Who places his glory and highest joy in God alone—
That he knows this Highest Good, that he pleases God!

Meditation 70

> *But the LORD is the true God; He is the living God and the everlasting King. At His wrath the earth will tremble, and the nations will not be able to endure His indignation. —* Jeremiah 10:10 (NKJV)

God alone is true; the world has show and lies.
Ah, trust in God's faithfulness—He will never deceive you!
Only God is living; your gold and goods are dead.
If God lives, He will also help you out of need.
What is visible passes away; only God shall remain forever.
To You, eternal King, I will forever bind myself.
Ah, only take my heart and make it Your throne;
Drive out all enemies utterly and dwell therein forever!

Meditation 71

> *Woe is me for my hurt! My wound is severe. But I said, "Truly this is an infirmity, and I must bear it."* —Jeremiah 10:19 (NKJV)

O sin, deceitful thing, you bring only bitter plagues;
Therefore must I now cry "Woe is me!" when I feel you.
I fell into murderers' hands, so that I see myself in blood;
I am stricken, sick and faint, and cry out only: Woe!
Take heart, O soul, you who feel sin's distress within your heart;
Think: God's wisdom thus slays sin through sin's own pains.
Bear your plague gently and still—you are yourself to blame—
And only wait upon God's help in humility and patience!

Meditation 72

> *O LORD, I know the way of man is not in himself; it is not in man who walks to direct his own steps. O LORD, correct me, but with justice; not in Your anger, lest You bring me to nothing.* —Jeremiah 10:23–24 (NKJV)

I know, and ever more experience, how easily I can waver;
Lord, let Your Spirit's discipline keep me within bounds!
My light and purpose suffice not; my powers are too small;
I, a weak and foolish little child, must be led by You.
I yield myself to Your hand and to Your wisdom's leading;
You can prepare me for Your kingdom through cross and suffering.
Well then, strike and chasten me—yet You know measure and limit;
Lord, do it not in Your wrath, and forsake me not utterly!

Meditation 73

> *Thus says the LORD to this people: "Thus they have loved to wander; they have not restrained their feet. Therefore the LORD does not accept them; He will remember their iniquity now, and punish their sins."* —Jeremiah 14:10 (NKJV)

Run here and there, O pious soul, in much outward exercise—
Such are not the best children whom our God would love!
You live scattered into this and that, disturbed evermore;
Therefore you become not aware of God and God's work within yourself.
The good children gladly stay at home with God in the heart,
And when they run here and there, they only get pain.
My Lord and Father, bring me home and hold me night and day,
That I, as Your dear child, may ever please You still!

Meditation 74

> *Have You utterly rejected Judah? Has Your soul loathed Zion? Why have You stricken us so that there is no healing for us? We looked for peace, but there was no good; and for the time of healing, and there was trouble. We acknowledge, O LORD, our wickedness and the iniquity of our fathers, for we have sinned against You.* —Jeremiah 14:19–20 (NKJV)

Have You rejected me, Lord? Shall I then perish in pain?
Am I now loathsome to You? Will You look on me no more?
You have so smitten me that none can heal me.
Ah, my Friend—if You Yourself smite me,
You my Savior—then heal me!
Parched Zion, mark it well: God rejects only your sins;
He is enemy to the Selfhood that is found within your Ground.
Hope here and hope there—believe it, your spirit finds no peace
Until you feel and freely confess that you are an evil child!

Meditation 75

> *Therefore thus says the LORD: "If you return, then I will bring you back; you shall stand before Me; if you take out the precious from the vile, you shall be as My mouth. Let them return to you, but you must not return to them."* —Jeremiah 15:19 (NKJV)

God gladly works all things in you—yet if this is to happen,
He would also see willingness and faithfulness on your part.
When one would turn to God, He helps that one can do it;
Only keep your desire weaned away; be still and wait then!
I turn to You, Lord, as I can, yet the true turning
Must Your inward drawing and Presence itself work and teach me.
Ah, become manifest to me in the spirit; if only this happens,
Then can I stand, turned inward, before Your countenance!

Meditation 76

> "And I will make you to this people a fortified bronze wall; and they will fight against you, but they shall not prevail against you; for I am with you to save you and deliver you," says the LORD. "I will deliver you from the hand of the wicked, and I will redeem you from the grip of the terrible." —Jeremiah 15:20–21 (NKJV)

Ah yes, then can the soul stand wholly secure and steadfast,
When she remains at home with God, and God within her inwardly.
Such a soul even the hellish tyrant fears;
Though he try, yet she shall not be overcome.
And though the soul walked in darkness and the Lord seemed far from her,
Yet God is and remains near to those who gladly remain with Him.
Even when the soul almost succumbs, God holds her fast in secret;
He snatches her out, and at last redeems her utterly from all sin.

Meditation 77

> "Behold, I will send for many fishermen," says the LORD, "and they shall fish them; and afterward I will send for many hunters, and they shall hunt them from every mountain and every hill, and out of the holes of the rocks. For My eyes are on all their ways; they are not hidden from My face, nor is their iniquity hidden from My eyes." —Jeremiah 16:16–17 (NKJV)

The fisher seeks only through sweet bait to catch the fish fast;
So do You, Lord, catch many a soul with sweet drawings of love.
Thereafter You send oft many hunters; the hounds run in;
One is plagued, one is hunted; one finds rest nowhere.
Yet, Lord, You are good in all; I will no more complain.

I will gladly let myself be fished; I will let myself be hunted.
Continue, and hunt Selfhood out of every corner—
Nothing can hide itself from You—so shall I find rest in the house!

Meditation 78

> *"Blessed is the man who trusts in the LORD, and whose hope is the LORD. For he shall be like a tree planted by the waters, which spreads out its roots by the river, and will not fear when heat comes; but its leaf will be green, and will not be anxious in the year of drought, nor will cease from yielding fruit."* —Jeremiah 17:7–8 (NKJV)

Trust not in outward things, in your own wit and works,
In good intention, light, and comfort—let God alone be your strength.
Trust in God with all your might, in faith alone, simply;
He remains standing when all falls—only turn inward into Him!
Ah, how blessed is the man who thus goes out from all
And stands rooted in God, like a tree planted by the brook!
In dry times and suffering's heat he remains as he was;
He draws from God the sap of life—therefore he is green evermore.

Meditation 79

> *For I heard many mocking: "Fear on every side!" "Report," they say, "and we will report it!" All my acquaintances watched for my stumbling, saying, "Perhaps he can be induced; then we will prevail against him, and we will take our revenge on him." But the LORD is with me as a mighty, awesome One. Therefore my persecutors will stumble, and will not prevail. They will be greatly ashamed, for they will not prosper. Their everlasting confusion will never be forgotten.* —Jeremiah 20:10–11 (NKJV)

Reason and flesh, and those who set themselves up as more than friends,
They watch and lure and think to fell me.
Because I fight them as enemies, they also seek revenge;
Their flattery is deceit and cunning—I care nothing for it.
Indeed I am blind and weak in myself and could so easily fall,
Yet You will be with me, my Lord, my mighty Champion, in all.
If You are near me with Your power, if You hold me by the hand,
Then the enemies' might is as nothing—they themselves fall in shame.

Meditation 80

> "Am I a God near at hand," says the LORD, "and not a God afar off? Can anyone hide himself in secret places, so I shall not see him?" says the LORD; "Do I not fill heaven and earth?" says the LORD. —Jeremiah 23:23–24 (NKJV)

You live and float ever in God; therefore seek Him not afar.
He sits not, in truth, shut up high above moon and stars.
Were you yourself not so far off,
So multiplied and distracted,
If you came rightly to yourself,
You would find God near in the spirit.
O near Essence, bring me near, that I in Your light
May walk in reverence, wherever I am, before Your countenance.
I will not hide myself—nay,
My heart lies bare; see how I mean it.
You fill earth and heaven, Lord—
Leave not my poor heart empty!

Meditation 81

> *"Then I will give them a heart to know Me, that I am the LORD; and they shall be My people, and I will be their God, for they shall return to Me with their whole heart."* — Jeremiah 24:7 (NKJV)

O most satisfying Good, O Essence of light and love,
Who knows You as he ought—who has it not from hearing and from reading—
Who turns his whole heart to You away from every creature:
To him You give also a heart, that he may know You only.
O Jehovah, who thus rightly knows You in Your light,
Gives himself willingly to such a God and burns in His love.
Lord, in humility I thank You that You have given me the mind
That such a God is my God, and that I am His.

Meditation 82

> *"For I know the thoughts that I think toward you,"* says the LORD, *"thoughts of peace and not of evil, to give you a future and a hope. Then you will call upon Me and go and pray to Me, and I will listen to you. And you will seek Me and find Me, when you search for Me with all your heart. I will be found by you,"* says the LORD, *"and I will bring you back from your captivity; I will gather you from all the nations and from all the places where I have driven you,"* says the LORD, *"and I will bring you to the place from which I cause you to be carried away captive."* —Jeremiah 29:11–14 (NKJV)

When God sets you in suffering and seems to forsake you,
Believe it—He has something good in mind; it is not meant for evil.
He seeks only your whole heart; He would make it small and pure,
That it may be free from sin and need, forever in peace.
Hear, Zion: though you are as one cast out and captive,
God will gather you again; you shall come home once more!
Then will you seek God aright and find Him near in the spirit—
This is the end indeed, for which you have long waited.

Meditation 83

> *The LORD has appeared of old to me, saying: "Yes, I have loved you with an everlasting love; therefore with lovingkindness I have drawn you."* —Jeremiah 31:3 (NKJV)

I, as the prodigal son, had taken myself far away
Into the world and Selfhood, far from God and His life.
To me, a straying creature, the Lord appeared there;
His love thought on me; His goodness drew me near.
Lord, who am I, that You have drawn me from the world to You?
Your goodness and free grace have moved my poor heart.
Yes, You have loved me from eternity, undeservedly;
Would that I now might also love You thus eternally, without self-interest!

Meditation 84

> *"For I have satiated the weary soul, and I have replenished every sorrowful soul." After this I awoke and looked around, and my sleep was sweet to me.* —Jeremiah 31:25–26 (NKJV)

Ah, I grow so faint and weary, walking such a way of the cross
Through the barren wilderness, where no path nor track is seen—
Poor and bare and hungry, wholly troubled and distressed,
Because I see myself still so far from Him whom my heart loves.

Weary soul, take comfort; God refreshes with a thousand gifts.
Yes, you shall yet be satisfied when you shall have Him Himself.
Only sink away from the creature; fall asleep into this death,
Until your spirit awakens in God—yes, the sleep shall be sweet!

Meditation 85

> *"Behold, the days are coming," says the LORD, "when I will make a new covenant with the house of Israel and with the house of Judah—not according to the covenant that I made with their fathers in the day that I took them by the hand to lead them out of the land of Egypt, My covenant which they broke, though I was a husband to them," says the LORD. "But this is the covenant that I will make with the house of Israel after those days," says the LORD: "I will put My law in their minds, and write it on their hearts; and I will be their God, and they shall be My people."* —Jeremiah 31:31–33 (NKJV)

In the beginning, when the Lord would bring His people out of Egypt,
He must mostly constrain them through conscience-fear and through the Law.
One leaves the evil only out of fear; one forces oneself to the good,
Yet the soul keeps not this covenant—the lust sits inwardly.
Lord, write Your law into my heart; give strength and desire and love
To follow freely and willingly the impulse of the new Spirit.
Make me a child of the new covenant; be You my God alone,
And let me be eternally faithful to You and wholly Yours!

Meditation 86

> *"Nor shall the priests, the Levites, lack a man to offer burnt offerings before Me, to kindle grain offerings, and to sacrifice continually."* —Jeremiah 33:18 (NKJV)

The Lord's priestly race shall never pass away;
It shall stand before His countenance at all times.
However much reason contradicts, though decay already sets in,
Yet inward souls shall always remain upon the earth.
O chosen souls, who desire nothing in the world
But to consume body and soul and all unto the Lord—
In love and praise and thankfulness they burn day and night;
Their offering for all is brought before God in the spirit!

Meditation 87

> *"And do you seek great things for yourself? Do not seek them; for behold, I will bring adversity on all flesh," says the LORD. "But I will give your life to you as a prize in all places, wherever you go."* —Jeremiah 45:5 (NKJV)

If one will give nothing more in the world to evil self-love,
Then the crafty serpent seeks her life within Christianity—
After great things she strives—after gifts and light and show;
One wishes for a high station; one would be something great.
O dear soul, desire it not! God loves the godly indeed,
Yet upon flesh and Selfhood must death and misfortune come.
Lord, Your glory delights me; for myself I seek nothing at all.
If You give me my soul for a prize, I am great enough.

Meditation 88

> *"But do not fear, O My servant Jacob, and do not be dismayed, O Israel! For behold, I will save you from afar, and your offspring from the land of their captivity; Jacob shall return, have rest and be at ease; no one shall make him afraid."* —Jeremiah 46:27 (NKJV)

So far into world and Selfhood have I gone from God;
In unrest, fear, and want my poor spirit sits captive.
When shall I finally find rest at home in the Father's bosom?
I struggle and sigh: "Lord, help me—else I shall never be free!"
Burdened soul, despair not; who believes, to him it shall succeed.
God speaks: "I will help you free; I will bring you back again
Out of yourself and your wretched state
Into Me, your true Fatherland."
There you shall close in secure rest
Your joyful eyes so gently!

Meditation 89

> *Thus says the LORD of hosts: "The children of Israel were oppressed, along with the children of Judah; all who took them captive have held them fast; they have refused to let them go. Their Redeemer is strong; the LORD of hosts is His name. He will thoroughly plead their case, that He may give rest to the land, and disquiet the inhabitants of Babylon."* —Jeremiah 50:33–34 (NKJV)

Sin, world, and Selfhood hold my spirit ensnared;
Ah, I am sorely plagued and oppressed by foreign power.
Though I struggle and though I cry,
Yet the enemy lets me not go free;
Ever I will and yet cannot—
I am a captive man.
Dear soul, despair not, were your state even ten times worse;
True, the enemy is too strong for you—but how strong is your Redeemer?
Let Him conduct your cause; He can do what no man can;
He breaks the hardest bond; He brings rest in the inner land!

Meditation 90

We would have healed Babylon, but she is not healed. Forsake her, and let us go everyone to his own country; for her judgment reaches to heaven and is lifted up to the skies. — Jeremiah 51:9 (NKJV)

How many have striven to heal Babylon again;
How many in zealous spirit would have torn her down!
Yet Babylon remains Babylon still; she shall never be healed.
God knows her great corruption well; God Himself will punish her.
Awakened souls, mark it well: you can spare yourselves the trouble.
Heal no more and strive no more; let Babylon quietly go.
Let each one only turn into his land and into his heart;
There mark and praise God's work, if you would be righteous!

Meditation 91

Then the glory of the LORD went up from the cherub, and stood over the threshold of the temple; and the house was filled with the cloud, and the court was full of the brightness of the LORD's glory. —Ezekiel 10:4 (NKJV)

Where God fills the heart—this purest Light of lights—
There the spirit worships Him in deepest darkness.
He tastes not this nor that; he has no visions either;
Indeed he tastes and sees God, yet without distinction.
Yet where the Godhead dwells in the house itself in darkness,
There the outer court grows full of His glory's splendor.
In the senses and the understanding the purest lights do sparkle;
Word and work and walk become a light in the Lord entirely.

Meditation 92

> *"As for your nativity, on the day you were born your navel cord was not cut, nor were you washed in water to cleanse you; you were not rubbed with salt nor wrapped in swaddling cloths. No eye pitied you, to do any of these things for you, to have compassion on you; but you were thrown out into the open field, when you yourself were loathed on the day you were born. And when I passed by you and saw you struggling in your own blood, I said to you in your blood, 'Live!' Yes, I said to you in your blood, 'Live!'"* —Ezekiel 16:4–6 (NKJV)

So it goes when the soul is born anew in the spirit:
She must first see herself rightly rejected and lost—
Rejected as a dead carcass that foully stinks,
Lost as a child lies in its blood in its last gasps.
So am I, Lord: You see me trodden down in my blood.
You speak indeed that I shall live, that You will rescue me,
Yet You pass by still. Come near to me, wretched one;
Speak once more with power into my heart: Soul, you shall live indeed!

Meditation 93

> *"Thus you were adorned with gold and silver, and your clothing was of fine linen, silk, and embroidered cloth. You ate pastry of fine flour, honey, and oil. You were exceedingly beautiful, and succeeded to royalty. Your fame went out among the nations because of your beauty, for it was perfect through My splendor which I had bestowed on you,"* says the Lord GOD. *"But you trusted in your own beauty, played the harlot because of your fame, and poured out your harlotry on everyone passing by who would have it... Therefore I have also diminished your rations, and given you up to the will of*

those who hate you, the daughters of the Philistines, who were ashamed of your lewd behavior." —Ezekiel 16:13–15, 27 (NKJV)

How precious is the adornment of the inward soul—
Her gentle and still spirit, her Essence unmoved!
The virtues and the graces are not to be numbered
Wherewith Jehovah Himself has adorned the worthy bride!
She has a kingdom; at the full table she sits;
Through God's glory she becomes perfectly beautiful.
Yet when she leans upon herself and her own beauty
And makes herself common—O woe, how shall it go!

Meditation 94

"Nevertheless I will remember My covenant with you in the days of your youth, and I will establish an everlasting covenant with you. Then you will remember your ways and be ashamed, when you receive your older and your younger sisters; for I will give them to you for daughters, but not because of My covenant with you. And I will establish My covenant with you. Then you shall know that I am the LORD, that you may remember and be ashamed, and never open your mouth anymore because of your shame, when I provide you an atonement for all you have done," says the Lord GOD. —Ezekiel 16:60–63 (NKJV)

When the Law punishes you for sin, you would fulfill it better,
Yet the covenant cannot still God's justice nor your conscience.
Sin only becomes more sinful; there is no other Ground
Than Jesus' blood, which blots out sins according to God's covenant of grace.
Yes, Lord, I think on it still and must be silent in shame
That You forgive me all my sin and will take it from me.
By grace, without my merit, I am now to be Your child;
Ah, so I learn that You are Lord and Savior alone.

Meditation 95

> *"I will make you pass under the rod, and I will bring you into the bond of the covenant; I will purge the rebels from among you, and those who transgress against Me; I will bring them out of the country where they dwell, but they shall not enter the land of Israel. Then you will know that I am the LORD."* —Ezekiel 20:37–38 (NKJV)

No king is found here so free and so content
As souls whom the bond of love has joined with God in the spirit,
Who, free from lust for the creature and thoroughly will-less,
Ever inwardly yield themselves to God and follow Him simply.
Lord, bring me, Your rebellious child, also into this bond of the covenant;
Make me faithful to the words of Your mouth through Your rod of discipline.
Let Your staff of the cross wholly slay what else lives in the heart,
Until all is swept out of me that still resists You!

Meditation 96

> *"Thus says the Lord GOD: 'Remove the turban, and take off the crown; nothing shall remain the same. Exalt the humble, and humble the exalted. Overthrown, overthrown, overthrown, I will make it overthrown! It shall be no longer, until He comes whose right it is, and I will give it to Him.'"* —Ezekiel 21:26–27 (NKJV)

How ready is Selfhood to claim all things for itself!
If one has left the filth of this world in first repentance,
One calls oneself in one's own mind
Already Christ's bride and queen,
And with the cap of freedom covers
The abomination that yet lurks in the Ground.

Ah, this is far from being she—lift off the crown to the earth!
You must be brought to nothing, nothing, nothing, and deeply humbled!
Of him who thinks himself to be, God speaks:
"This soul also is not the one."
Who is wholly stripped and small and lowly—
He alone has the right to the crown.

Meditation 97

> "She has grown weary with lies, and her great scum has not gone from her. Let her scum be in the fire! In your filthiness is lewdness. Because I have cleansed you, and you were not cleansed, you will not be cleansed of your filthiness anymore, till I have caused My fury to rest upon you." —Ezekiel 24:12–13 (NKJV)

We never become wholly holy through activity alone.
Exert yourself through this and that—your heart will not become pure.
The bottom is wholly burned on; the evil sits in the Ground.
You must, you must go into the fire, else it will never be known to you!
You cannot become thoroughly cleansed from your Selfhood
Unless you feel the Lord's wrath in the cross here on earth.
Lord, You would gladly purify me; my heart also gladly wills it.
Give grace, then, that I may hold still for You in suffering!

Meditation 98

> "Then I will bring you down with those who descend into the Pit, to the people of old, and I will make you dwell in the lowest part of the earth, in places desolate from antiquity, with those who go down to the Pit, so that you may never be inhabited; and I shall establish glory in the land of the

> *living. I will make you a terror, and you shall be no more; though you are sought for, you will never be found again," says the Lord GOD.* —Ezekiel 26:20–21 (NKJV)

When Adam would exalt himself, the beauty of his soul faded.
When Christ humbled Himself to the cross, to the grave, and to hell,
Then was the beauty restored,
The land of the living opened.
Who now would see the beauty there
Must also go down with Him.
Who gets a little light and grace would unawares rise like Adam.
My God, how deep must one then bow to the grave in that wilderness,
Bereft of life and comfort and light,
Until one has become utterly nothing!
There first becomes the land of the living
And its beauty known in the Ground.

Meditation 99

> *"Say to them: 'As I live,' says the Lord GOD, 'I have no pleasure in the death of the wicked, but that the wicked turn from his way and live. Turn, turn from your evil ways! For why should you die, O house of Israel?'"* —Ezekiel 33:11 (NKJV)

Think, soul: this is God's Word; the mouth of the Lord swears
That He, as surely as He Himself lives, desires not your death!
Were your ruin ever so great, only trust—there is no danger.
Hear: God has no pleasure even in the death of the godless.
Only turn from the heart; leave your way and will.
God loves you; He desires it so; He will also fulfill it Himself!
Nay, Jesus, I will not die; I believe what Your Word promises.
Only give me then what You require; live in me, that I may live!

Meditation 100

> *"I will feed them in good pasture, and their fold shall be on the high mountains of Israel. There they shall lie down in a good fold and feed in rich pasture on the mountains of Israel. I will feed My flock, and I will make them lie down,"* says the Lord GOD. *"I will seek what was lost and bring back what was driven away, bind up the broken and strengthen what was sick; but I will destroy the fat and the strong, and feed them in judgment."* —Ezekiel 34:14–16 (NKJV)

Ah, feed me in You with You, my good Shepherd;
Let Your heart be my fold and gentle resting place.
Seek the lost soul; bring back again the straying one;
Bind up and strengthen Your sick and weak little sheep!
Let another freely suppose that he is something and can do something;
Destroy utterly in me the fat and strong mind.
Grant that I may deeply know my Nothingness and Your grace—
That You are my good Shepherd and I Your little sheep!

Meditation 101

> *"You are My flock, the flock of My pasture; you are men, and I am your God,"* says the Lord GOD. —Ezekiel 34:31 (NKJV)

I am a man of dust and earth, and You my God and Lord;
Before You I remain but poor, though I were holy, still.
I am a man—yet I am Yours;
Yes, Lord, I am Your lambkin.
Lead me unto Your pasture-place,
For You are God, and I Your sheep.
True, I am man and sinner too, who oft withstands Your will—

A weak and foolish creature, prone to wander in the wrong.
Yet You are God, and have long patience;
Your grace and favor bear me up:
My unfaith cannot make Your faith
So quickly turn away from me.

Meditation 102

> *"But you, O mountains of Israel, you shall shoot forth your branches and yield your fruit to My people Israel, for they are about to come. For indeed I am for you, and I will turn to you, and you shall be tilled and sown."* —Ezekiel 36:8–9 (NKJV)

Lord, speak to my dry Ground, which yet can bear no fruit:
"I am for you; I turn to you; I would bless and till you."
Let me believe and hope that better days shall come,
That You will plough and plant this barren land.
My people are about to come—the powers of the new life;
Then shall my branches shoot and bear their fruit.
Only be for me, my God, and turn Your face to me;
So shall even this wilderness become a fruitful field.

Meditation 103

> *"Then I will sprinkle clean water on you, and you shall be clean; I will cleanse you from all your filthiness and from all your idols. I will give you a new heart and put a new spirit within you; I will take the heart of stone out of your flesh and give you a heart of flesh. I will put My Spirit within you and cause you to walk in My statutes, and you will keep My judgments and do them."* —Ezekiel 36:25–27 (NKJV)

Sprinkle me, O God, that I may be clean;
Wash all my filthiness and idols away.
My heart is stone—it cannot feel Your love;
Give me a heart of flesh, tender and new.
Put Your Spirit within me; let Him work and move
That I may walk in all Your ways.
Without this gift I cannot keep Your law;
Do You Yourself in me what You require!

Meditation 104

> *Again He said to me, "Prophesy to these bones, and say to them, 'O dry bones, hear the word of the LORD! Thus says the Lord GOD to these bones: Surely I will cause breath to enter into you, and you shall live. I will put sinews on you and bring flesh upon you, cover you with skin and put breath in you; and you shall live. Then you shall know that I am the LORD.'"* —Ezekiel 37:4–6 (NKJV)

The means of grace are like the sinews in the frame;
The outer flesh and skin are doctrine, works, and duties—
Which even a dead heathen may perform by nature.
I live not as a Christian while I stay in this alone.
It is the Spirit that I lack—else nothing helps me, truly;
'Tis seeming without being, a corpse without a life.
God must bestow on me Christ Jesus' Spirit within,
That I may live as Jesus lived, and know His power indeed.

Meditation 105

> *Also He said to me, "Prophesy to the breath, prophesy, son of man, and say to the breath, 'Thus says the Lord GOD: Come from the four winds, O breath, and breathe on these slain, that they may live.'" So I prophesied as He commanded me, and breath came into them, and they lived, and stood upon their feet, an exceedingly great army.*
> —Ezekiel 37:9–10 (NKJV)

God slays by Law, and by a thousand trials of suffering;
There sinks the spirit oft quite down into sheer death and faintness.
God also makes alive by His own power from above;
His Spirit raises up the dull, weak sense of faith.
Look not to East nor West, if this must be in you;
Turn inward, and lie still before God—as one that is dead.
Soon shall a gentle Spirit breathe through the quiet Ground,
And His peace-power revive again both heart and courage.

Meditation 106

> *Then He said to me, "Son of man, these bones are the whole house of Israel. They indeed say, 'Our bones are dry, our hope is lost, and we ourselves are cut off!' Therefore prophesy and say to them, 'Thus says the Lord GOD: Behold, O My people, I will open your graves and cause you to come up from your graves, and bring you into the land of Israel. Then you shall know that I am the LORD, when I have opened your graves, O My people, and brought you up from your graves. I will put My Spirit in you, and you shall live, and I will place you in your own land. Then you shall know that I, the LORD, have spoken it and performed it,' says the LORD."* —Ezekiel 37:11–14 (NKJV)

My heart is dried and withered—without sap and strength and life—
Like some dead bone that lies there, cold, insensible.
This faintness presses me almost to cast away all hope;
A severed limb, men say, receives no life again.
Lord, therefore help me Yourself—since it is at an end with me;
Bring me out of the grave; break every bond of death.
Only send Your Spirit of life with power into my heart—
So shall I live before You, in You—my true Land.

Meditation 107

> *The Spirit lifted me up and brought me into the inner court; and behold, the glory of the LORD filled the temple. Then I heard Him speaking to me from the temple, while a man stood beside me. And He said to me, "Son of man, this is the place of My throne and the place of the soles of My feet, where I will dwell in the midst of the children of Israel forever."* —Ezekiel 43:5, 7 (NKJV)

Lift me up, O Spirit-wind, above the world, and nature, and the senses;
Bring me into the inward place—for else I never enter in!
Deep in the Ground—there it is fair;
There one can see, as with the eyes,
How the Lord's glory-splendor
Fills this house entirely.
Inward—beyond both place and time—is the place ordained for Your throne.
Make the Ground, my King, made clean; come dwell therein forever!
Spirit and soul, and heart and mind
Fall down at Your feet.
Reign in me—drive all things out;
Fill this house wholly with Yourself!

Meditation 108

> *Also He brought me by way of the north gate to the front of the temple; so I looked, and behold, the glory of the LORD filled the house of the LORD; and I fell on my face. And the LORD said to me, "Son of man, mark well, see with your eyes and hear with your ears, all that I say to you concerning all the ordinances of the house of the LORD and all its laws. Mark well who may enter the house and all who go out from the sanctuary."* —Ezekiel 44:4–5 (NKJV)

God would in fatherly kindness stoop unto His children;
Their pure Ground shall be His house, His temple, and His home.
Yet reverence soon teaches one to bow within
When His Majesty enters into this house.
Devoutly must the heart, with all the inward senses,
Be turned still and inward toward God's voice.
The inward law shows how to serve God in the spirit,
And teaches entrance and departure in this sanctuary.

Meditation 109

> *"But the priests, the Levites, the sons of Zadok, who kept charge of My sanctuary when the children of Israel went astray from Me, they shall come near Me to minister to Me; and they shall stand before Me to offer to Me the fat and the blood,"* says the Lord GOD... *"It shall be, in regard to their inheritance, that I am their inheritance. You shall give them no possession in Israel, for I am their possession."* —Ezekiel 44:15, 28 (NKJV)

Each walks his way according to the light he has received;
Great is the difference even among the devout.
The priestly race that stands before the Lord—
The inward people—has no possession here.

Their inheritance is the Lord, to whom they've wholly given themselves;
And Him they possess, in essence, in the Ground.
They have in nothing else but God any delight or life;
One only is their portion—and it abides forever.

Meditation 110

> *"All the way around shall be eighteen thousand cubits; and the name of the city from that day shall be: THE LORD IS THERE."* —Ezekiel 48:35 (NKJV)

"The LORD is there"—so call I such a soul,
Who has become as dead to every creature,
Who chooses nothing for delight but God alone,
Whom many trials of the cross have made both small and pure.
So comes Jehovah then, and dwells within the soul's own Ground;
The tabernacle of God draws near to men.
One sees God in the spirit, bowed low at every hour—
And from that day she bears the name: "The LORD is there."

Meditation 111

> *Nebuchadnezzar the king made an image of gold... Then a herald cried aloud: "To you it is commanded, O peoples, nations, and languages, that at the time you hear the sound of the horn, flute, harp, lyre, and psaltery, in symphony with all kinds of music, you shall fall down and worship the gold image that King Nebuchadnezzar has set up; and whoever does not fall down and worship shall be cast immediately into the midst of a burning fiery furnace." Shadrach, Meshach, and Abed-Nego answered and said to the king... "Our God whom we serve is able to deliver us from the burning fiery furnace... But if not, let it be known to you, O king, that we do not serve your gods, nor will we*

worship the gold image which you have set up." —Daniel 3:1, 4–6, 16–18 (NKJV)

The hellish tyrant, prince of this world,
Has set before our reason and our sense,
From without and from within, unrolled
Full many a golden idol for offense.
He can subdue the world, when shrill
His pipes and pompous music ring;
Only my heroes bend not still—
Three men yet stand, who trust their King.
They look not on the images, but God;
Lord, make me likewise faithful unto You,
In need and death: far rather let me burn
Than ever other gods to know or see!

Meditation 112

And at the end of the time I, Nebuchadnezzar, lifted my eyes to heaven, and my understanding returned to me; and I blessed the Most High and praised and honored Him who lives forever... At the same time my reason returned to me, and for the glory of my kingdom, my honor and splendor returned to me. My counselors and nobles resorted to me, I was restored to my kingdom, and excellent majesty was added to me. —Daniel 4:34, 36 (NKJV)

I was the king himself—by pride thrust out,
From pleasure, land, and station—made a beast,
Plagued in dull unreason, with false lust about;
How glorious once I stood—now crawled, despised, least!
Lord, when shall these seven times have end,
Till I my deep Nothing learn, and Your great might?
When only unto heaven humility's eyes bend,
Then grow I wise, and fair, and bright as once in light.

Meditation 113

Now I, Nebuchadnezzar, praise and extol and honor the King of heaven, all of whose works are truth, and His ways justice. And those who walk in pride He is able to put down. — Daniel 4:37 (NKJV)

How secretly can Selfhood shine in light and gifts!
Then men praise God, so long as He complies with their desire;
They call His ways most right where their own seeing lifts,
But in the dark vale of suffering begins the censor's fire.
Yet, Lord, You can abase—You cast from throne to ground,
And make a foolish, poor beast Your own child and king;
He honors You as King, and counts himself but bound:
Your doing is all truth; Your ways are right in everything.

Meditation 114

Now the king was exceedingly glad for him, and commanded that they should take Daniel up out of the den. So Daniel was taken up out of the den, and no injury whatever was found on him, because he believed in his God. —Daniel 6:23 (NKJV)

Like an anxious lions' den is this world to the godly,
Wherein they ever meet temptations, snares, and fears;
Satan goes round; the world-spirit roars out boldly;
Wrath, sin, and Selfhood—evil beasts—are near.
How shall I, feeble lamb, escape these dangers so,
Since by my own strength and wit I never can be sure?
I let go self and creature; You alone I trust—
O keep me in this dark house, and draw me forth secure!

Meditation 115

> *"Those great beasts, which are four, are four kings which arise out of the earth. But the saints of the Most High shall receive the kingdom, and possess the kingdom forever, even forever and ever."* —Daniel 7:17–18 (NKJV)

In heaven the saints reign; on earth, great beasts hold sway;
Who here would be both great and mighty is one of these.
A saint lives here unknown, in lowly servant's way;
The world's realm comes and goes—his kingdom never flees.
If you from vanity be weaned, and wholly hallowed unto God,
The Most High gives you His own kingdom in the soul's Ground:
His eternal splendor—throne and crown—while flesh and world are but His sod,
A footstool underfoot. Where you are no saint, you are no king renowned.

Meditation 116

> *"Now therefore, our God, hear the prayer of Your servant, and his supplications, and for the Lord's sake cause Your face to shine on Your sanctuary, which is desolate."* —Daniel 9:17 (NKJV)

How desolate am I—God seems so far from spirit;
My heart, His house and sanctuary, stands full of abominations!
O blissful countenance, my God, come help and visit;
Shine on my dark Ground, O fair dawn of consolations.
Let Your gracious Presence in the spirit be seen once more;
Fill all my soul's deep Ground, as Your own temple wholly.
There dwell and reign as pleases You; there let me stand before
You, Lord, till Your face's splendor change me to Your image, meek and lowly.

Meditation 117

> "For how can this servant of my lord talk with you, my lord? As for me, no strength remains in me now, nor is any breath left in me." Then again, the one having the likeness of a man touched me and strengthened me. And he said, "O man greatly beloved, fear not! Peace be to you; be strong, yes, be strong!" So when he spoke to me I was strengthened, and said, "Let my lord speak, for you have strengthened me." —Daniel 10:17–19 (NKJV)

O highest Majesty—must I have speech with You,
When the man "greatly beloved" sinks down in faintness sore?
And yet I fear not, for You look on me
In human form, that beckons graciously once more.
You have become the Son of man, and come to me as mild,
That I may freely see and hear You in my heart.
Speak then, my Lord—You have taken away my fear;
Yes, speak, till I be made that "greatly beloved" part!

Meditation 118

> Then I heard the man clothed in linen, who was above the waters of the river, when he held up his right hand and his left hand to heaven, and swore by Him who lives forever, that it shall be for a time, times, and half a time; and when the power of the holy people has been completely shattered, all these things shall be finished. —Daniel 12:7 (NKJV)

You searchers of the times, mark signs of latter days,
When shall be fulfilled the wonders men rehearse.
Believe it: Christ prepares not for you His kingdom's blaze
So long as heart and mind from Him are scattered—worse.
Reckon not wrongly—writing numbers, years, and dates;

Bring the Many into One; stand still within the Now.
He who is wholly unified within, and waits,
May in himself the thousand-year realm taste, and wonders know.

Meditation 119

> *"Many shall be purified, made white, and refined, but the wicked shall do wickedly; and none of the wicked shall understand, but the wise shall understand."* —Daniel 12:10 (NKJV)

The wheat may lightly yet be cleansed from chaff, it's true;
It is not enough, though from dead works you clean appear.
Through and through within you sits earth's filthy hue;
The lye bites sharp, ere you be snow-white, pure, and clear.
Nor is it ended: gold itself must pass the fire;
Deepest soul-distress reveals the worst dross in the Ground.
My Refiner, press on—make me in trials truer,
And many with me too. Blessed he that wins the crown!

Meditation 120

> *"But you, go your way till the end; for you shall rest, and will arise to your inheritance at the end of the days."* —Daniel 12:13 (NKJV)

See, reader, here the close of writing and of reading:
The end of all is this—go to the End, and rest.
This was the writer's aim, wisdom's true leading
In this small play of rhyme: seek you the same, and be blest.
God is your End alone, where rest is found indeed;
Go out from self and every creature unto Him.
So work-less rest in stillness; let images recede—
Then shall you find what here I write. I seek it too—still, dim.

PART II: VERSES ON CHRIST'S ASCENSION

A Supplement of Short Verses on the Power of Christ's Exaltation Written for the Day of His Ascension

1. Gifts for All

> *You have ascended on high, You have led captivity captive; You have received gifts among men, even from the rebellious, that the LORD God might dwell there.* —Psalm 68:18 (NKJV)

So take I courage nonetheless, for Jesus triumphs.
The victor's gifts, which He received without measure,
Are for us men indeed—and not for the godly only;
He has something even for me, though I have rebelled.

2. The Everlasting Redemption

> *Not with the blood of goats and calves, but with His own blood He entered the Most Holy Place once for all, having obtained eternal redemption.* —Hebrews 9:12 (NKJV)

My High Priest enters into the Holiest;
Forever He has reconciled the multitude of my sins.
Come, sinners—love God; you may find redemption;
Yet must your sin be drowned in Jesus' blood!

3. The Promised Spirit

> *Nevertheless I tell you the truth. It is to your advantage that I go away; for if I do not go away, the Helper will not come to you; but if I depart, I will send Him to you.* —John 16:7 (NKJV)

A cloud bears up the Fountain of all life;
How richly now shall heaven's clouds rain down,
And bless faint hearts with grace, with Spirit, and with comfort—
Lord, overflow me with the baptism of Your Spirit!

4. The Prize Set Before Us

> *Looking unto Jesus, the author and finisher of our faith, who for the joy that was set before Him endured the cross, despising the shame, and has sat down at the right hand of the throne of God.* —Hebrews 12:2 (NKJV)

Deny with good courage the base delight of earth;
Despise shame and mockery; endure the burdens:
Soon all is past—look only unto the glory
Which Jesus there possesses, and what He here has done.

5. The Heavenly Mind

> *If then you were raised with Christ, seek those things which are above, where Christ is, sitting at the right hand of God. Set your mind on things above, not on things on the earth.* —Colossians 3:1–2 (NKJV)

Then there is nothing more on earth for my spirit;
My heavenly Magnet touches me and draws me.
My heart, my mind, my longing—He will have for Himself:
Where my treasure is, there must my heart be found.

6. The Reconciling Intercession

> *My little children, these things I write to you, so that you may not sin. And if anyone sins, we have an Advocate with the Father, Jesus Christ the righteous.* —1 John 2:1 (NKJV)

I must be as a little child, and not grieve the Father;
A little child in suffering, doing, and loving;
And though I fall into mire, I still must be His child,
For with the Father I have my pure Brother.

7. The Constant Nearness of Jesus

> *Teaching them to observe all things that I have commanded you; and lo, I am with you always, even to the end of the age.* —Matthew 28:20 (NKJV)

I see this and that—and yet should see but One:
You, Jesus, Friend, abide near, though You seem to go.
Grant that I childlike believe, when I neither see nor feel,
That You are with me every day—and even now.

8. The Final Victory

> *But this Man, after He had offered one sacrifice for sins forever, sat down at the right hand of God, from that time waiting till His enemies are made His footstool.* —Hebrews 10:12–13 (NKJV)

Though all my foes rage on, at last they must
Bow—even in me—beneath my King's feet.
He waits upon the throne; His waiting teaches me
In faith and patience to wait likewise here.

9. Jesus, Lord of Hearts

> *Therefore being exalted to the right hand of God... Therefore let all the house of Israel know assuredly that God has made this Jesus, whom you crucified, both Lord and Christ.* —Acts 2:33, 36 (NKJV)

Hear, all Israel, and rejoice no little:
Him whom you crucified is now your Lord and King!
I am Your subject, O Lord of highest spirits—
Ah, be, and remain, my heart's own Lord and Master!

10. The Glorifying of Jesus' Name in Us

> *But made Himself of no reputation... Therefore God also has highly exalted Him... that at the name of Jesus every knee should bow.* —Philippians 2:7, 9–10 (NKJV)

If I be brought to nothing, God shall raise me up:
So was it, Jesus, with You—so must it be with me.
Yet no—remain You high: I in Your Name will bow
With reverence, love, and joy, forever. Amen.

11. The Indwelling of Jesus

> *He who descended is also the One who ascended far above all the heavens, that He might fill all things.* —Ephesians 4:10 (NKJV)

My Jesus would ascend above the heavens,
That He might bow most inwardly unto my heart.
I should be His heaven—He is so near to me:
Come, Jesus, take me in; come, fill me wholly with Yourself!

12. The Sanctuary Opened

> *Therefore, brethren, having boldness to enter the Holiest by the blood of Jesus... let us draw near.* —Hebrews 10:19, 22 (NKJV)

In Jesus' blood the veil is now taken away:
The greatest sinner may, and can, and must come in
Unto God's sanctuary. Go then, O soul—draw near,
Through dying and through prayer unto this deep repose.

13. Translation into the Heavenly Life

> *And raised us up together, and made us sit together in the heavenly places in Christ Jesus.* —Ephesians 2:6 (NKJV)

Translated must I be—messengers and gifts cannot suffice;
With coming and with going Love will not be fed.
Ah, Jesus, lead me home; You can restore and heal me:
Translate me wholly with Yourself into the heavenly life!

14. Kept in Love

> *Now I am no longer in the world, but these are in the world, and I come to You. Holy Father, keep through Your name those whom You have given Me, that they may be one as We are.* —John 17:11 (NKJV)

To You, Lord, we are given—do You also keep us,
According to Your last petition! Let love not grow cold;
Let us be one—cleaving to You in quietness of spirit;
Let us be one—enfolded in love.

15. The Glorifying of the Body

> *For our citizenship is in heaven, from which we also eagerly wait for the Savior, the Lord Jesus Christ, who will transform our lowly body that it may be conformed to His glorious body.*
> —Philippians 3:20–21 (NKJV)

This body of lowliness presses me well-nigh to earth;
It weighs upon my spirit with more than one burden.
O Jesus, Glory, one day shine through all that is old,
And fashion even this dark body like unto Yours.

16. Our Place Prepared

> *In My Father's house are many mansions; if it were not so, I would have told you. I go to prepare a place for you. And if I go and prepare a place for you, I will come again and receive you to Myself; that where I am, there you may be also.* —John 14:2–3 (NKJV)

Here it is never right with me; here I find rest nowhere.
When shall I reach the place, Lord, which You have prepared,
Where, beyond place and time, I shall be led into You?
In heaven there is no place for my spirit but You.

PART III: ON THE HOLY LOVE OF GOD

Original Translator's Preface

An unbidden impulse lately pressed upon me, at an unseasonable hour—when head and eyes were dull—to render into German what Madame Guyon writeth here; I did what I could; what I could do stands here.

Whether my rendering be faithful, each may judge, if he know French, and the language of Love; he must also understand something of the craft of rhyme; yet if God but count it good, then have I done it well.

What thou canst not grasp is not written for thee; what leadeth thee not unto God, thou understandest not aright. One doth not weigh words when hearts love fervently—Lord, would that I were wholly filled with this pure flame!

Original Author's Preface

In these leaves is shown the great distinction betwixt false worldly love and pure Love: how blessed is the man who liveth in dependence upon God's Love—nothing burdeneth him, nothing boweth him down!

Even the greatest pains become to us sweet and lovely when one beareth them willingly, and for God's sake; how pleasant is the sharpest anguish and torment where this fair flame is cherished in the heart!

The pleasures of this world are full of bitterness: one is disturbed, confused, and ever as in restless bustle; let a man compose himself as best he may, seek far and near—the heart remaineth burdened, and fast in the vise.

Only Thou, O Love of God, givest the fulness of joy; Thou makest our hearts simple, gentle, and peaceable; but whoso yieldeth himself as prey to false love, even in the midst of mirth feeleth, at bottom, nothing but pain.

Let us therefore here behold the great difference—whether one belongeth unto God, or be a slave of sins: for they who walk their way in holy innocence, their hearts are weaned from what is to be found below.

A slave of sins is plagued by his tyrant: he hath no rest; his best "joy" is torment; with loathing and vexation evil lust gnaweth at him—he lieth as in the mire of vices, past all numbering.

But the slave of my God findeth himself ever most free; nothing presseth his heart, nor bringeth it as into a prison: pure Love delivereth him from sin, from wicked appetite and lust that spring from hell.

Therefore let us follow boldly the track of pure Love; let us despise false love and its imagined pleasure; let us hate its way, and deny Nature—pure Love shall in the end overcome it.

Yea, dearest Love, to Thee—only to Thee—belongeth the victory: we can do nothing of ourselves, save only resist Thee; since one triumphs only through Thee, O Love, to Thee must all, and the whole honour, be given.

THE SPIRITUAL FLOWER GARDEN

The Holy Love of God and Unholy Natural Love

(From Madame Guyon, rendered into German by Tersteegen)

Poem 1

> *Behold, I will send for many fishermen, says the LORD, and they shall fish them.* —Jeremiah 16:16 (NKJV)

O Love of God—go fish, ah, fish so many hearts,
That sensual lust may catch not one;
Its bait brings only sorrow; Your bait is divine—I bite it willingly.
See to it, sweet Fisher, that no heart slip from You;
Hold fast those already taken;
Snatch them all away from the deceiver!
My blessed gain, my happiness is only this:
That my heart be never torn from Your hand—
O blessed lot, O sure estate!
My God, my Bridegroom, how it would delight me
If I might see my heart lie there with those before You!
With steadfast, faithful love I would gladly ever remain near You.

Poem 2

> *Sharp arrows of the mighty, with coals of the broom tree!* — Psalm 120:4 (NKJV)

O holy Love of God, how glad I am
When I behold Your arrow fly!
Ah, might my wish succeed—
That it would strike me and pierce my heart right through.
It is done—yes truly; my heart is already slain:
The dearest Master's arrow hits true.
So long as I stood high upon the perch,
I feared the arrows of another.

Victorious hand of Almighty power,
You will keep from dangers
What You have conquered.
Blind world-love, with bandaged eyes,
Cannot look up into the heights.
Away, vain love: your false delight
Shall nevermore deceive my heart!

Poem 3

Do business till I come. —Luke 19:13 (NKJV)

In vain you show me your wares:
The sweet poison of frantic vanity,
As though it were your richest booty,
Beguiles me not—I let it pass.
You blind not those hearts
To whom God's Love promises shelter.
Cross, nails, and thorns are fairer unto me;
What you display is but vapor.
The favor of the Most High God,
And grace without number,
He gives in their stead;
The scourges—and all that belongs
To Jesus' cross—are precious in my eyes.
Go, seek another to seduce,
For I am already my Bridegroom's,
And this is my fixed intent:
To adorn my head with His crown.
His cross is my heart's delight;
No sweeter good do I know.
To You, O Love of God, I yield myself;
Let my lot be in Your hand.
I trust Your faithfulness;

I am content to suffer while I live,
And bear Your crown of thorns—
Spare me not, even unto death.

Poem 4

> *And the pride of Israel testifies to his face, but they do not return to the LORD their God, nor seek Him for all this.* —Hosea 7:10 (NKJV)

Nothing is more hateful to the highest Love of God
Than cherished, empty pride.
The Friend—and he whom He loves—
Both wage war against pride, till it be wholly slain.
No: you never please God in loftiness;
Humility draws Him down unto the soul.
Would you taste purely the sweetness of Love,
Then remain small—bowed down—brought low.
The Highest keeps Himself far from all high estate;
In the deep valley His little spring wells up.
Nothingness and yielding lowliness draw Him,
That He may gladly fill a poor heart with delight.
The Bridegroom heaps goods into the bride's bosom—
Let us then live ever in self-abasement.
To deep lowliness He will give, as its proper portion,
Pure Love of God;
And then the soul perceives the voice of the Eternal Word,
Which otherwise no other can.

Poem 5

> *But those who desire to be rich fall into temptation and a snare, and into many foolish and harmful lusts which drown men in destruction and perdition.* —1 Timothy 6:9 (NKJV)

That poverty of spirit which Jesus taught us
Preserves us from the enemy's snares;
He lays his snares for those who stoop toward riches,
And makes a man scarcely enjoy half of what is allotted him.
With how much unrest and confusion, early and late,
Must one guard that perilous "good"
With burden, sorrow, and dangers!
Far nobler is the treasure which God's Love possesses.
Yes—this Love gives itself at once
To him who yields up all for it;
And if one loves it wholly pure,
It becomes the soul's own support—its firm ground.
Beloved poverty, be you wholly my riches!
In you one tastes power and truth,
Peace, and the clarity of wisdom.
He forfeits this great good who grasps at empty glitter.

Poem 6

> *Jesus answered them, 'Most assuredly, I say to you, whoever commits sin is a slave of sin.'* —John 8:34 (NKJV)

Unhappy is the man whom lust drives on,
For he remains the slave of pleasures;
Where he thinks to satisfy the craving,
There the enemy mocks him in mad self-deceit.
But You, O Love of God, make blessed—here and there—
When one in freedom serves You;
Your tenderest taste so binds us
That even in suffering we find something excellent and fair.
A bondman of sin and flesh lives here in constant pain,
And bears hell already in his bosom.
Ah, cease your sinning,
Else shall the hell that is here drive you into that hell beyond.
Had you but tasted the chaste delight of Love
Wherewith God fills a pure and faithful soul,

However far your desire might stretch,
Soon—more than you think—it would be fulfilled.
Believe me: yield yourself to God,
That His Love alone may live within your heart.
He who burns in this fair fire
From henceforth knows a joy that is eternal.

Poem 7

> *Not lagging in diligence, fervent in spirit, serving the Lord.* —
> Romans 12:11 (NKJV)

So lukewarm in Christianity, so sluggish unto prayer—
This cannot please my Lord.
Learn then to conduct yourself more wisely,
And serve the highest Majesty with better earnestness!
This is false rest; this "stillness" deceives.
Far otherwise are God's ways:
One runs after the Bridegroom; the heart is fresh and light;
One follows Him everywhere along the thorny path.
Love and the cross—on these alone we lean;
For such a way God chooses.
All else is but devotion's mask—
A dead image and a show of piety;
In truth, mere deceit and foolishness.
So one serves not God; so one follows Nature.

Poem 8

> *Deliver me from the guilt of bloodshed, O God, the God of my salvation, and my tongue shall sing aloud of Your righteousness.* —Psalm 51:14 (NKJV)

How exceedingly sick—how wretched am I!
And daily it grows worse.
Only through Yourself can I be healed,
You Object of my love, You divine Being of Love!
Tender Physician, spare not my blood;
Draw off all that does harm;
Deliver me wholly from evil and burden—
I shall serve You better, when I am made whole.
I am but foul corruption—
Weakness and poverty itself;
A marsh, full to be named of unclean vapors;
The truth of what I am I must yet better learn.
Your only medicine for me is Your Love:
Pour it deep into my Ground.
When pure Love at last possesses my heart,
Then shall I live wholly sound—without weakness, without pain.

Poem 9

> *O LORD, do not rebuke me in Your anger, nor chasten me in Your hot displeasure... Remember, O LORD, Your tender mercies and Your lovingkindnesses, for they are from of old.*
> —Psalm 6:1; Psalm 25:6 (NKJV)

Have I then, great God, awakened Your wrath,
That so terrifies me, most miserable?
How have I dared to displease You, my God?
Even to think on it is pain.
I have indeed deserved to feel Your lightnings;
Yet consider, Lord—what would it profit You?
I am but poor dust of the earth,
Not even worth Your jealous zeal.
A pure nothing am I—will You show punishment on such?
Well then, my Lord, I will bow down.
I consent unto Your righteous sentence:
This faithless, thankless heart shall be my own abhorring.

Let Your wrath sink down, my Lord and King;
I adore Your chastening rod.
Do what You will—it shall seem sweet to me;
Only forget what evil I have done!
Though I displeased You but for one moment,
I am worthy that punishment press me hard.

Poem 10

> *Have I sinned? What have I done to You, O watcher of men?...*
> *Look upon me and be merciful to me, as Your custom is*
> *toward those who love Your name.* —Job 7:20; Psalm
> 119:132 (NKJV)

Go not away, my Bridegroom;
In You alone I hope, my Lamb.
Behold my faith, behold my grief;
Let Your Love be moved toward my heart.
Flee not—You see my pain:
No fire nor torment can afflict me so.
Lord, punish me according to Your strictness—
Your blows drive me not into such straits as this.
No, Love—no: I cannot bear it
That You should withdraw—O bitter going from me!
I would rather lose my life;
It grieves me—return; be not torn from me!
Fie on my sin—I hate it unto death.
Only behold my woe, my deep suffering!
I could depart out of this life—
Yet no: I fear no distress;
In the greatest anguish I will live content,
If only You, my God, my Dearest, will forgive me.

Poem 11

> *That they might know that by what things a man sins, by these he is punished... Now Absalom happened to meet the servants of David. Absalom rode on a mule. The mule went under the thick boughs of a great terebinth tree, and his head caught in the terebinth.* —Wisdom 11:16; 2 Samuel 18:9 (NKJV)

You show me aloft a child in rebellion;
With loathing I behold the warning.
If I should prove unfaithful unto You,
More loathsome yet would I be in Your sight, my God.
How, Father-heart—ah, have I mocked You?
You, who have crowned me with benefits;
You, who have broken my bonds—
To offend You—O shame, O foul disgrace!
Could floods of tears but soften You—
Could I, through all pain, attain
That You would again be gracious unto me—
I would count myself most blessed.
How blessed then would I count myself even in suffering;
I would yield myself with joy unto the hardest punishment;
Only when You are angry—ah—then must my sorrowing heart
Perish in need and pain.

Poem 12

> *Are not my days few? Cease! Leave me alone, that I may take a little comfort... Since his days are determined, the number of his months is with You; You have appointed his limits, so that he cannot pass.* —Job 10:20; Job 14:5 (NKJV)

My God, my Dearest, remember:
My short days pass away like a shadow.

In this dark house here,
If it please You, a fair day may dawn for me.
Your nearness is the well of light;
Your absence makes me find only night.
Give full brightness, O Sun of grace;
Enlighten my soul—kindle my weary heart!
If Love but break my bonds,
I care not, nor grow pale at death.
Though the hour be unknown to me,
I yield myself the more to the Highest Good.
My Bridegroom, forgive—ah, forgive:
My days are as nothing—You know it.
To You I give myself, my love;
Bear me as my support in weakness.
Though I have but few years remaining,
Yet can You use them for Your honor.
When once my body falls into the grave,
Then shall my heart praise You without end with yonder choirs.

Poem 13

> *Put on the whole armor of God, that you may be able to stand against the wiles of the devil.* —Ephesians 6:11 (NKJV)

With weapons of faith must one stand well armed,
If one would meet the enemy.
Come—only keep near to the King,
Who drives him away with a look!
This short life is the true time of battle:
Overcome the devil—and Nature too!
The negligent are quickly struck down;
Who can bear so dreadful a ruin?
If one follows the enemy, he cannot belong to God;
Think not that such a thing is possible.
He who would cleave to God but by halves
Is unfit to obtain grace.

As Jesus walked, so must we go step by step
And follow on to Calvary;
Else can one receive no soldier's pay,
Nor with Him be decked in triumph.
O adorable Captain, my Head—go You before;
I follow Your banner of the cross!
He who fights under Your oversight
Fears no severity, but beats down the foes.

Poem 14

> *God is wise in heart and mighty in strength. Who has hardened himself against Him and prospered?* —Job 9:4 (NKJV)

Far rather would I yield myself a captive to Your hand
Than strive against You.
The glory of such "braveries"
Suits ill with my estate.
I must, my Bridegroom, fight only against myself,
And submit to Your blows;
Else would I be overbold indeed,
And justly would Your wrath be kindled.
Ah Lord, the victory is Yours—take You my weapons!
I will contend only against Your enemy,
Not against Your thousand kindnesses,
To which my heart and all are subject.
You great God, I will then be Your prisoner—
Yes, from my whole heart.
This great blessedness I will never squander;
I would rather suffer every pain.

Poem 15

> *But I will deliver you in that day, says the LORD, and you shall not be given into the hand of the men of whom you are afraid... because you have put your trust in Me, says the LORD.* —Jeremiah 39:17–18 (NKJV)

Lord, behold the soul that sits in captivity:
The devil and the flesh have barred door and crack.
Since You have so loved me—ah—
Deliver me, for none else can.
O God, whom my spirit worships and honors:
If You set me free from this, my prayer is heard;
Then by Your truth yet make me,
Day by day, more free.
Tear me out of the enemy's chains;
Let me never—never—step back into the net,
That I should fall and perish—permit it not!
Not half—but wholly blessed—You make.
Hold me near You without turning aside;
Let my heart love You; let it worship You continually.
You are my Bridegroom alone;
You alone pour in such grace.

Poem 16

> *These things I have spoken to you, that in Me you may have peace. In the world you will have tribulation; but be of good cheer, I have overcome the world.* —John 16:33 (NKJV)

So now the enemy lies dead through Your goodness,
And troubles me no more;
Pure Love has won the battle,
And with sure victory has subdued false love.
Holy Love of God drives every other love far off;

One feels the great distinction.
O inconstancy—one must grow pale,
That an ungrateful heart could ever forsake Love!
I fear not that lust should take new life again:
You have too well defeated it.
It lies cast down at Your feet;
My Love, I fear not that it shall plague me again.
I follow only after You, and cleave to You most inwardly;
I follow You as long as I live.
Suffer me not to be lukewarm and slothful,
Nor spare, my Lord, Your faithful strokes upon me,
Till I be pliant, gentle, and low,
And made truly fit and becoming unto You.

Poem 17

> *The sacrifices of God are a broken spirit, a broken and a contrite heart—these, O God, You will not despise.* —Psalm 51:17 (NKJV)

You, Love, would have my whole heart—
Lo, here I bring it You instead of other gifts;
Ah, take it from my hands!
It is done: to You I leave it,
And have delivered it in best wise;
No higher happiness can ever be to it.
If You accept my offering, ah, then suffer it
Never again to be snatched from Your hands.
Love will not refuse me, surely,
What here I have besought.
Because You take my heart, it is wholly Yours;
Lose not Your own possession.
Let all Your floods rather break upon my head,
O King of my heart, Lamb of God:
Sufferings are sweet to me; the hardest will I bear,
If only You will be my Bridegroom.

Poem 18

Having disarmed principalities and powers, He made a public spectacle of them, triumphing over them in it. —Colossians 2:15 (NKJV)

In the Cross alone does Love triumph,
Where pain, where thorns pierce through us;
So has my Jesus Himself chosen it—
This is the very way whereby God leads souls.
As Jesus goes, so follow Him unwavering;
Look only on our banner—let Jesus and His fair Cross
Stir us to zeal!
A poor and naked heart
Is fitted well for the Cross.
Away with delay, away with vain deceiving!
We would surrender even our very selves;
We shall live truly well-content,
If we embrace the hardest cross without fear.
Blessed is he who on the pilgrim way
Follows unwavering the banner of pure Love.

Poem 19

No one can come to Me unless the Father who sent Me draws him; and I will raise him up at the last day. —John 6:44 (NKJV)

Then draw me—draw me more mightily;
I follow You, my Lord, with courage.
The Cross bestows a twofold fruit:
It makes faith pure, and so increases love.
In Jesus' armor I prevail here;
Without it I should not come to You.
I—feeble—must needs faint,

And could not follow the sweet Bridegroom.
You draw me, great God, with Your strong drawings,
And lift body and soul unto Yourself.
How soon would my flame fly out,
If Your drawing came not to help me!
I ascend unto You, adorable Good,
Because I am upheld by Jesus' cross and blood.
Your drawing, O Father, is precious to my heart;
Yet for it I thank Your Son's sufferings.
I thank His blood; I thank His life:
The more strongly You do draw me,
The more the soul sinks down into You,
The more must I give thanks unto Jesus, the Beloved.

Poem 20

> *Catch us the foxes, the little foxes that spoil the vines, for our vines have tender grapes.* —Song of Solomon 2:15 (NKJV)

Come, Love of God, to drive forth wholly from my soul
All Selfhood that disorders and torments me;
Teach me Your truth;
Pour Your sweet fire into me!
I was the vineyard itself, so blooming to behold;
You would tend it day and night, and build it up;
The enemy, alas, let foxes in—
A stumbling-block to You, O Love.
When foxes run to and fro, and burrow in the earth,
The fairest plants are utterly troubled and made foul.
Selfhood makes war on Love,
And is a thief of Love's children.
Root out this evil breed, my Lord,
So contrary to the great good You would lay within our soul!
Selfhood corrupts outright
What once was in the Bridegroom's garden.
You may call it mother—fruitful in wickedness—

That ever bears children (who can number them?);
A spring whence every sin wells up;
Its offering God holds abominable.

Poem 21

You put my feet in the stocks, and watch closely all my paths. You set a limit for the soles of my feet. —Job 13:27 (NKJV)

How, Love—would You now keep me with chains,
To hold me near to You?
You could spare your labor as needless,
For faith and love already bind me.
Would You lay fetters on my feet, as though I purposed
Wherein I cannot even walk?
My heart and soul long since are slaves and Yours—
Why then would You bind me so?
I need no chains, O Ruler of my life,
Save the bond of Your pure Love.
The chains You would else lay on me are in any case in vain—
Ah, do not put this shame upon me!
Fasten me to the tree of the Cross—why torment me otherwise?
Bind me to no other tree.
If You, my Friend, approve not my well-meant choosing,
My spirit feels only necessity and constraint.

Poem 22

He has bent His bow and set me up as a target for the arrow. — Lamentations 3:12 (NKJV)

My heart is as a mark, toward which You ever let fly
Your arrows, glowing-hot.
I grow too faint; I must give over—
If You love me, then hold Your hand!

Yet no—it is grief to me; I knew not what I said.
Shoot on, You sweet Love; I stand;
I heed not my vain fear—
The Bridegroom's arrows do not hurt.
Shoot on, shoot on, my Lord, whom I alone adore;
Henceforth call my heart the mark of Your arrows.
Wound it—let it be wholly Yours;
Grant that I may love You and know You.
You cleave my heart, my Salvation;
So piercing is Your arrow.
Do You deal thus, O dear Conqueror,
With souls that are wholly Yours—Your faithful, loving children?

Poem 23

> *You have ravished my heart, my sister, my spouse; you have ravished my heart with one look of your eyes, with one link of your necklace.* —Song of Solomon 4:9 (NKJV)

You—when You wound us—say that one wounds You:
The saying is wholly hidden from me.
Let Your wisdom one day, with a divinely true mouth,
Teach me what lies within its meaning.
Yea, yea—I now grasp this high mystery:
The selfsame arrow wounds You too
Wherewith You gave Your bride her wound—
This is the deep sense and ground.
Rather exchange heart for heart: give to the bride Your own!
Nothing more lovely can be.
She has her heart no more; henceforth she would see only
The Bridegroom's heart within herself.
And she has full right, the bride, in her desire,
In this exchanging of hearts with You;
For thereby love is founded firm forever,
And every fear departs from her.

Poem 24

As gold in the furnace He tried them, and accepted them as a burnt offering. —Wisdom 3:6 (NKJV)

Then lay the heart into the furnace,
That it be changed and made pure;
Let this holy fire transform it—
Else give a new one for this old!
Yea, with eager courage I desire
To see my heart within this glow.
Quickly, O Love, hear my petition:
Lay it into the furnace—into the midst!
Show me this grace. Your fire has something truly delightful;
The glow of Love refreshes my heart—
I have a pleasure in the pain.
Form my heart after Your manner;
Make it pure and true, and tender inmost-wise.
Wholly let it be Yours—yea, in the best way—
And let Your Love remain forever sure.
O Love, consume my heart, and grant
That I may love with Your Love.
The highest power is in Your hands—
Therefore do You soon complete this work!

Poem 25

Take away the dross from silver, and it will go to the silversmith for jewelry. —Proverbs 25:4 (NKJV)

My heart is infected with rust
Through Selfhood, small and great.
When You bestow gifts on me,
I soon defile them; Lord, lay my heart bare unto Your truth!
Grind on, until the rust be gone;

Lay hold upon the heart; turn the stone—
Yet no: it helps me not; a new one must You form in me,
Wherein there is nothing human; the heart must be divine.
Another way were far shorter:
Cast the heart into the glow of Your furnace;
Let the fire of Your Love consume the whole heart—
For no other fire works such an effect.
True, water flows from my eyes
To wash my faithless heart;
Yet without this holy fire it is of little worth:
Without Love it soon lies again in mire and pain.

Poem 26

> *Like an apple tree among the trees of the woods, so is my beloved among the sons. I sat down in his shade with great delight, and his fruit was sweet to my taste.* —Song of Solomon 2:3 (NKJV)

O sweetest Love, graft Your Cross into my heart;
Yea, let it there take root!
I choose this tree above all trees—
From it much grace of God does spring.
The nails, the thorns, the pains and sufferings that I meet
Are fruits of the Tree of Life;
Yet they are sweet only to Your beloved,
Who have wholly pledged their soul to You.
You, Love of God, make their suffering taste
As a fruit of lowliness.
They who truly hearken to Your voice
Disturb the vain softness of the flesh.
One grows great-hearted and despises evil opinion;
One loves God purely, without guile.
There He is King of our hearts;
One fears all enemies but little.

Poem 27

> *Rejoicing in His inhabited world, and my delight was with the sons of men.* —Proverbs 8:31 (NKJV)

Soul. Dearest Love of God—why do You play here?
Jesus. I play with the bride, to teach you:
The world we (she and I) ever toss to one another,
And secretly we laugh at what others love.
Soul. Who shall win between us two,
And who in this play shall suffer loss?
Jesus. He who loses gains much
In all our love-play.
Soul. The very contrary was in my mind;
I thought I must have with You nothing but gain.
O dearest Bridegroom, explain this mystery to me—
Ah, grant my request!
Jesus. If one "wins" with Me, and possesses Me even here,
How can he hold Me—Me, who am wholly unbounded?
If you lose yourself in Me, and your love depart not from Me,
Then can you not perish, sunk with Me into oneness.
Soul. With You I will lose everything upon earth—
My own as well.
Sink me deep into Your bosom!
If I may be wholly the dear Master's own,
Then shall I praise forever this my most blessed lot.

Poem 28

> *I have been crucified with Christ; it is no longer I who live, but Christ lives in me; and the life which I now live in the flesh I live by faith in the Son of God, who loved me and gave Himself for me.* —Galatians 2:20 (NKJV)

Soul. I thought I had long since reached the goal of blessedness;
The dear Master already was mine.
Now I behold myself lying in pain and suffering;
It seems that Love can deceive a little after all.
Jesus. Why do you complain? I give you much good;
Now will I fashion you otherwise.
Abide in My bonds, and let Me deal with you—
You must be made conformable unto Me.
I suffered a thousand torments, that you might not perish;
And you—you fear the least pain.
You cannot be Mine without suffering and without dying;
Consider only My patience in suffering!
Soul. Forgive it, O Love of God! I adore Your smiting.
I was afraid, because I knew it not.
Now the blows are sweet to me; I will gladly bear them,
Nailed to the Cross by the dear Master's hand.
This also comes to me: Suffering must indeed be lovely,
Since You have given me this high lesson to consider—
That without the Cross no good on earth is worthy to be prized.
Blessed are we, if You will help us
To this wood whence life does spring—
A wood that destroys all sin, and wins for us
A salvation—an eternal salvation which no envy ever spoils.

Poem 29

> *I charge you, O daughters of Jerusalem, by the gazelles or by the does of the field, do not stir up nor awaken love until it pleases.* —Song of Solomon 3:5 (NKJV)

No, no—I fear no more the world with all its power;
The devil cannot wound me,
Nor can hell nor death affright me;
Torment and martyrdom I heed not.
In safety do I live; in quiet I fall asleep;
Love makes me without care.

It watches for me in my slumber;
It makes me sure.
I know of no anxiety; in no fear do I hover.
In incomparable sweet peace,
From evil and from good set apart,
I live in the world as one alone.
I see only Love; I know it only.
I am as a stranger to all doing;
It is my support and strength;
It lightens every load and pain.

Poem 30

Praise Him with the timbrel and dance; praise Him with stringed instruments and flutes! —Psalm 150:4 (NKJV)

O excellent music—O fairest harmony
Of Bridegroom and bride—how glad are he and she!
You give her, Lord, a foretaste of the heavenly singing;
You play, the soul sings—what can sound sweeter?
O adorable Good, my Master, would that I might here
One day sing the divine song with You as well!
Take my will—take my inmost heart—my very being:
Oh teach me; strike on—Your strokes are chosen indeed.
The harmony must be fair; the playing must be excellent,
When our will enters into Your will.
The sweet melody can be heard only in God—
He finds it who loses himself in Him without return.
Then one accords always, though the notes be many;
This is the beauty of singing and of playing:
The more the tone is changed, the more the soul rejoices,
And shows obedience and faithfulness.

Poem 31

> *Because of the fragrance of your good ointments, your name is ointment poured forth; therefore the virgins love you. Draw me away! We will run after you.* —Song of Solomon 1:3–4 (NKJV)

If one but follow You in blindness, O pure Love,
How safely do we walk!
Through Reason's eye we wander from the path;
In faith's dark night we go on without light—
Yet seldom now it comes to pass
That any on that fair way is rightly led.
Men trust the senses; naked, pure believing they refuse;
The senses lead us astray—Love only leads aright.
The more she makes poor and strips bare,
The more she takes all and leaves nothing unto us,
The more the heart receives wider room:
It goes straight unto the goal, and stumbles not, nor wavers, nor drifts;
Its portion is pure Love, and still remains so—
This is the heart's whole business; else it loves not, or hardly.

Poem 32

> *For I am hard-pressed between the two, having a desire to depart and be with Christ, which is far better.* —Philippians 1:23 (NKJV)

How bitter is death to him that loves not aright!
How sweet, O Lord, to him that loves You alone!
Then is it full of grace—more than one would suppose;
He waits for it without fear, as for a true good thing.
O Death, you give life unto us, and awaken it,
And hide in your bosom thousand temptings.
You loose bonds, and out of thousand miseries

Your hand makes free what, ere death, would slay us.
While I am on the earth I still may sin;
Still may I lose my God out of my mind:
But Death brings all good, and is the end of all my woe,
And leads me into the good land—into God's kingdom and His hands.
Therefore I love you, O Death—yea, after you I long;
Who shall yet grow pale—whom can you yet affright?
Not the heart, truly, that has poured itself wholly into God,
But the faint heart indeed, that neither believes nor loves.
O blessed moment, wherein one doubts not!
O happy day, that breaks what is natural!
Day full of peace, that shows me nothing hard;
O day that abides ever, and never inclines unto night!

Poem 33

> *Behold, you are fair, my love! Behold, you are fair! You have dove's eyes. Behold, you are handsome, my beloved! Yes, pleasant!* —Song of Solomon 1:15–16 (NKJV)

We lay aside the mirror, my God, my Love, for now;
I mirror myself in Your clearness.
Only You would I behold, O highest Truth—
Myself forget, and live without one backward glance.
That I should yet find myself is intolerable unto me;
I would see my God alone.
You whom I love, adore, and own—
Ah, why am I still here? why do I find myself?
Destroy me—live You in Yourself alone;
Let me be found no more; You only must one see!
If, O great God, Love stand in the highest degree,
Then must one lose it—what can be sweeter?
To see oneself, to gaze, and boast that one loves You,
Is self-deceit, and never true:
A man must wholly forget himself,

Else without cause he only talks of himself.
A self-lover says he loves my Master—
I believe it not, though he be bold as bold may be.
If you love Him, show your faithfulness:
Let Him be your only good, and your whole stay.

Poem 34

> *But he who is joined to the Lord is one spirit with Him.* —1 Corinthians 6:17 (NKJV)

Melt into One, into One only, my heavenly Bridegroom,
So inwardly Your heart and mine,
That nothing more appear but Your heart alone—
O blow upon the fair flame!
In Your forge turn hearts a thousandfold;
Smite my heart till Your anvil ring;
Make it quite nought—how fair shall that be then!
If ever Your fire seem to die, make straight a new glow.
A heart like Your heart—yea, that there be but one heart:
When shall I taste this blessedness?
Let all hearts flow into One
Through a pleasant pain!
He that yet fears Your heat knows it not indeed;
Therein I find my pleasure.
Is true peace else to be obtained,
Where this dear necessity has never been tasted?

Poem 35

> *But whoever drinks of the water that I shall give him will never thirst. But the water that I shall give him will become in him a fountain of water springing up into everlasting life.*
> —John 4:14 (NKJV)

O divine Water, springing up unto eternal life,
That quenches every fleshly burning,
And fills us with taste of purest delight—
Ah, all else is but vapor!
You make our soul consume away
And ever die to all her craving.
Flow, gentle Water—flow—to fill the Ground of the soul;
You turn into flame, so sweet, so tender:
When You enkindle my heart, You can also still the thirst.
O high word of wonder—sweet transformation—
Whereby water became fire, and fire became cooling!
If you would search the Ground of this,
Learn only to find your salvation in pure Love.

Poem 36

> *Who forgives all your iniquities, who heals all your diseases.* —Psalm 103:3 (NKJV)

Sick and full of misery, yet I come—ah, be
My healing and my medicine.
Drive the enemy out of my heart;
Possess You this heart, and dwell therein forever.
Wash it in Your blood—so shall it be clean again,
Though it be never so defiled.
Nothing shall I feel hard or heavy,
If only You will wholly overcome Nature in me.
The world has beguiled me—deceitful, false it is;

I will deny its craft,
And leave the deceiver,
And gladly take up Your cross as my delight.
Ah, now I first perceive in what a night of blindness
I lived beneath its power;
Now I follow Jesus without turning,
And to be His alone I long with my whole desire.

Poem 37

> *For whom He foreknew, He also predestined to be conformed to the image of His Son, that He might be the firstborn among many brethren.* —Romans 8:29 (NKJV)

Then paint Yourself, and press Yourself into my heart,
You pattern, divinely fair, that ravishes my soul.
Drive out all spirits that would beguile me;
With Your pure flame of Love enkindle it!
When shall it be, my God, that I have You alone,
And no other pattern more appear?
My heavenly Bridegroom, paint indeed Yourself by grace into my heart!
I love nothing but You—chief pattern of my faith;
The whole world I account as vanity.
My Lord, my King—You only are;
I feel how deep my wretchedness is.
Love's burning lifts me indeed toward You;
Yet still my misery is not forgotten:
Night and day one thing returns to my mind—
My dearest Father's goodness only.

Poem 38

> *Let God arise, let His enemies be scattered; let those also who hate Him flee before Him.* —Psalm 68:1 (NKJV)

Ah, my own sweeping helps me not,
For Satan ever fouls the place anew with filth.
I yield it up—I know no counsel:
To You, O Love, and to Your pure grace I give myself.
I mark it: the more I sweep, the more I make it foul;
I grow confounded at the thing.
O come to my help, O Lord,
Else would my pain be overmuch!
I see You come, and with strong hand You will strike down
The enemy, and drive the shameful one away.
How thankful is my heart for such grace—
Show it fully by the deed!
Henceforth I must no more endure the foe before me;
If only I be with You, he must needs avoid me.
Be You my only stay,
My Master whom I honor—unto You I yield myself.

Poem 39

> *Oh, do not deliver the life of Your turtledove to the wild beast!*
> *Do not forget the life of Your poor forever.* —Psalm 74:19
> (NKJV)

I fear not, my Love, so many beasts' rage;
Lions and bears shall be for my salvation.
In You and in Your cross I shall find strength enough:
If they tear me, yet shall I overcome.
Spare me not—grind me, destroy me freely,
Till nothing of "mine" remain.
Then shall I be unfeigned—wholly pure in all—
And rightly please my King.
Their teeth must be as a mill,
To grind me small as grain,
Till I go forth from out their mouth
Like purest flour, fit for my Friend.
Knead me and bake me—put me in the oven—

That I may be a dish for You, my Lord.
The faithfulness of my Love desires this one thing only:
That whatsoever of Nature yet is in me be consumed.

Poem 40

> *O Jerusalem, wash your heart from wickedness, that you may be saved. How long shall your evil thoughts lodge within you?*
> —Jeremiah 4:14 (NKJV)

How unclean do I behold myself—ah me!
I look upon my great distress:
So poor am I, so weak—
But You, O Lord, in whom I trust, You can cleanse me.
Your precious blood is unto me
A holy vessel for washing—an open bath of grace:
Therein I sink all sin and harm,
That I may be acceptable before You.
Though I had sins as many as the sand of the mountains,
Not to be numbered,
In Jesus' blood I find cleansing
In all the sufferings that torment me.
This divine basin gives me rest and courage;
What else were heavy becomes light; the burden vanishes away;
My heart feels true largeness
In this pure, highest Good.
Why then do men delay, to bathe so often and so freely
In this most noble pool?
O excellent medicine—
You make my heart glad, and heal all the harm.

Poem 41

> *Sustain me with cakes of raisins, refresh me with apples, for I am lovesick.* —Song of Solomon 2:5 (NKJV)

You Yourself, O Love of God, have nailed me to the cross;
I cannot complain thereof.
I fear it not—nay rather I love the light burden,
When I consider that You did choose the cross.
I feel not its hardness;
It is a bed of joy—
A bed so full of purity,
As though one had sweetness instead of suffering.
Strike on my body—yet spare not; yea, strike on:
Nothing shall move me down from this Tree of Life.
Fasten me firm—You have nails enough;
I must die thereon, till my soul be ravished,
And from the cross fly up into my God's bosom!
Cross, you are great to my soul.
From this place will I never depart,
Till dying at last I reach the cross's reward.

Poem 42

> *He said to him again a second time, 'Simon, son of Jonah, do you love Me?' He said to Him, 'Yes, Lord; You know that I love You.' He said to him, 'Tend My sheep.'* —John 21:16 (NKJV)

My God, my Shepherd, come—help You Your flock:
The wolves press hard into Your sheepfold.
They snatch away a poor little lamb;
I pray You, ah, come ere all be laid waste!
You have oft commanded me that I should feed the sheep;
O You, in whom one ever finds the fairest pasture,
Ah, lead You them Yourself—else are they doomed to death!
A wolf, full of fury, comes there to tear them.
Ah, You have slain him—fear is gone from me.
Now, dearest little sheep, come—feed without dread;
Follow your Shepherd—follow with constancy:
With Him abundance and all good is found.

Go not astray—follow always in His steps;
Then shall you live beneath His leading
So sweet, so full of loveliness—
O Love, let me ever follow You so likewise!

Poem 43

> *I said, I will water my best garden, and will water abundantly my garden bed: and, lo, my brook became a river, and my river became a sea.* —Sirach 24:31 (NKJV)

Plant, O Love of God—plant in my heart Your cross and Your love;
Else would the earth bear other things.
I planted this little blossom; You come and water it—
This means something higher.
Yet this I thought herein as well:
Whatsoever grows in this world,
I desire not, nor call mine;
What earth and sea can give I despise,
That I may love You only.
To be taken up with You is my desire alone;
Nothing here beneath can please the senses.
If I be purely subject unto You,
How quietly shall I lie in Your arms!
Here I find what truly delights me;
Down there one cannot have it so.
The world counts this one thing a plague,
Wherein my heart refreshes itself with loveliness.
The world's way is far removed from Your track;
Your way is hidden from it, and bitter:
But I know this one thing only—
That with my Friend, with Jesus, I may live and die.

Poem 44

I in them, and You in Me; that they may be made perfect in one, and that the world may know that You have sent Me, and have loved them as You have loved Me. —John 17:23 (NKJV)

The end of pure Love is—to become one with God;
Love leads thither by ways full of hardship,
By suffering, cross, and shame—not by renown and honor:
This is the holy way—what would one have more?
God only! One Love makes all to be one;
The highest good is laid into that single point.
Love brings us into our own true origin,
Where our Beginning—God—does bear and move us.
O lofty unity of God, wherein the Bride then stands!
At last a divine mingling comes to pass.
The soul has nothing, yet is glad and steadfast of mind,
Transformed by Love into her highest Good.
One sees not that the Bride—the dearest—does appear any more;
God only works in her.
In her unity she is so utterly annulled,
That Love and Truth are seen—and nothing else besides.

When Jesus' Shepherd's Staff Leads Us

The glorious kingdom of Jesus Christ upon earth

> The wolf also shall dwell with the lamb, the leopard shall lie down with the young goat, the calf and the young lion and the fatling together; and a little child shall lead them. The cow and the bear shall graze; their young ones shall lie down together; and the lion shall eat straw like the ox. The nursing child shall play by the cobra's hole, and the weaned child shall put his hand in the viper's den. They shall not

hurt nor destroy in all My holy mountain, for the earth shall be full of the knowledge of the LORD as the waters cover the sea. —Isaiah 11:6–9 (NKJV)

When Jesus' shepherd-staff does lead,
The tiger lays aside his rage;
At His mild Spirit's gentle beck
The lion lets his fury sink;
The wolf becomes a little lamb,
A mighty man, a child, and small.
Come, golden time—fill you the earth—
That there be one flock, and one Shepherd!

Conclusion

Hear what the profit of all this ought to be:
That, without reservation, one should be God's—and love.
A twofold gain thereby does come to us,
Which till this hour was yet unknown.

Then, when we love God—who is our point of rest—
Then shall we find in Him the highest repose;
For pure Love suffers no other love beside,
Therefore must what in love is defective disappear.

In the Highest Being the heart lays itself to rest,
In the fairest Object that draws Love unto itself—
Who in Himself abides, and never moves,
Yet rules in wisdom all that is created.

His tender drawing of love draws the heart continually;
The drawing is unseen, yet so mightily inclines,
That though the sense, being gross, cannot well feel it,
Yet it shows itself more powerful than even death.

We yield ourselves then wholly unto His dominion,
Despite all the senses' rage—they cannot wound the Ground.
At the beginning one suffers, as it were, a martyrdom;
But Love a thousandfold at last will it repay.

GLOSSARY OF KEY TERMS
FOR THE ENGLISH EDITION OF GEISTLICHES BLUMENGÄRTLEIN (1729)

This glossary explains essential theological and mystical vocabulary that appears throughout Tersteegen's writings. Many of these words carry technical meanings within the Rhenish mystical and Reformed Pietist tradition. They cannot be reduced to modern psychological or sentimental equivalents.

Detachment (*Abgeschiedenheit*)

A spiritual separation from worldly attachments, images, and desires. In Tersteegen's theology, detachment is not emotional withdrawal but an interior turning away from the creaturely so the soul may turn fully toward God. It is the negative movement that complements yieldedness.

Distraction (*Zerstreuung*)

The scattering of the soul away from God through noise, activity, or inward division. The opposite of recollection. Tersteegen portrays the spiritual life as a constant battle against the soul's tendency to disperse itself among creatures and sensory experiences.

Essence / Being (*Wesen*)

God as the only true Reality. Contrasted consistently with illusion or mere appearance. Employed frequently in mystical theology to speak of God's essential nature. The soul seeks union not with God's works or gifts but with His very Being.

Ground of the Soul (*Seelengrund*)

A technical mystical term originating with Meister Eckhart. The deepest point of the soul, untouched by creatureliness, where the soul meets God. Capitalized throughout this translation to mark it as a doctrinal concept. Tersteegen urges readers to "sink into the Ground" where God dwells.

Hiddenness (*Verborgenheit*)

The mystery of God's presence that is veiled to the senses but revealed inwardly to the simple and yielded soul. Tersteegen frequently speaks of God's "hidden love" and calls believers to live "hidden in God"—unknown to the world, known only to the Father.

Images (*Bilder*)

Mental or devotional images that stand between the soul and God. Tersteegen warns against relying on images, insisting that true devotion is imageless and inward. The soul must become "free from images" to receive God's direct impression.

Inmost Heart (*Gemüt*)

The unified center of the human person—heart, will, and affections together. The place where God speaks. Never rendered as "mind." It is deeper than intellect and broader than emotion, the seat of the soul's orientation toward or away from God.

Inwardness (*Innigkeit*)

A depth of heart directed toward God. Not emotional warmth but interior attentiveness. True devotion arises from inwardness, not outward forms. The quality of being deeply present to God in the soul's center.

GLOSSARY OF KEY TERMS

Nothingness (*Nichts*)

A paradoxical mystical expression: as the self diminishes into nothingness, God becomes all in the soul. Never rendered as nihilism or psychological emptiness. "Through the nothing, nothing, nothing" runs the path to union with God.

Reason (*Vernunft*)

Human reason unaided by faith, often portrayed negatively as an obstacle to union with God. Never rendered as "wisdom." Tersteegen contrasts the restless questioning of reason with the peaceful simplicity of childlike faith.

Recollection (*Sammlung*)

The gathering of the soul's scattered faculties into unity before God. The opposite of distraction. The soul must be "gathered" from its dispersion among creatures to attend wholly to God in the Ground.

Self-denial (*Verleugnung*)

The deliberate renunciation of one's own desires, thoughts, and self-rule in order to follow Christ. Distinguished from negative forms of self-rejection; it is voluntary surrender to divine love. Tersteegen calls self-denial "the soul's bread" for the pilgrim journey.

Self-hood (*Eigenheit*)

The false, self-asserting identity that must be surrendered in order for the soul to be united with God. Associated with self-will, spiritual pride, and the desire to possess or control one's life. Never translated as "identity" or "ego." "The slightest self-hood is worthy of hell."

Self-will (*Eigenwille*)

Human willfulness set against God's will. Considered the root of sin in Tersteegen's theology. Not willpower or volition in general, but the stubborn assertion of one's own desires. The chief obstacle to yieldedness.

GLOSSARY OF KEY TERMS

Shadow / Illusion (*Schein*)

The unreality or deceptive appearance of the world in contrast to God's Essence. Tersteegen routinely contrasts mere appearance with true Being: "The creature has appearance—I am the true Being," says Christ to the soul.

Simplicity (*Einfalt*)

The virtue of having a unified heart before God, free from duplicity, complexity, or inner division. Not naïveté. A hallmark of Pietist spirituality. The "single eye" that looks to God alone, without distraction or double-mindedness.

Stillness (*Stille*)

The cessation of self-activity and self-talk before God. Stillness is the precondition for perceiving God's inward presence. Not silence merely, but quietness of will. "God dwells in the stillness."

Turning Inward (*Einkehr*)

The movement of withdrawing from outward distractions in order to attend to God within. Not introspection or self-analysis, but recollected awareness of God's presence. Tersteegen's constant exhortation: "Turn inward"—for there God waits.

Will-lessness (*Willenlosigkeit*)

The state of having surrendered one's own will entirely to God. The fruit of yieldedness. "How blessed, when one's own will lies in God like a dead thing—still." Not passivity or indifference, but active consent to God's direction in all things.

Yieldedness (*Gelassenheit*)

The central virtue of the Rhenish mystical tradition. A willing release of self-will into God's will. It is active openness, not passivity; surrender, not collapse; divine rest, not relaxation. The German term is retained in some passages where translation would weaken its meaning.

ABOUT THE TRANSLATOR

Jarred Fenlason, D.Min., is a teacher and writer drawn to the voices of those who have crossed the threshold from knowing *about* God to knowing Him. He holds a Doctor of Ministry from United Theological Seminary, where his research focused on discipleship and equipping believers to encounter the power, presence, and love of God.

He is the author of *The Interval: The Brief Window that Shapes Your Eternal Soul* and *Encounter Discipleship: An Interactive Biblical Discipleship Program*. His translation of Gerhard Tersteegen's *Spiritual Flower Garden*—the first complete English edition—grew from years of collecting the writings of Christian mystics and spiritual guides whose words carried the weight of firsthand encounter.

His passion is to awaken believers to the eternal significance of ordinary days—and to the One who is shaping them for eternity.

Jarred lives in Charlotte, North Carolina, with his wife, Rochelle. They have three adult children.

ALSO BY JARRED FENLASON

THE INTERVAL

The Brief Window That Shapes Your Eternal Soul

What if eternal life has already begun—and the person you are becoming now is the person you will carry into forever? Challenging the "waiting room" mentality that treats earthly life as mere prelude, Fenlason argues that the brief window between conversion and death is an unrepeatable interval of grace where believers lay up treasure in heaven and form the souls who will steward it eternally.

Available at Amazon.com

www.intervalbook.com

—

ENCOUNTER DISCIPLESHIP

An Interactive Biblical Discipleship Program

An 8-session interactive small group program designed to equip believers to encounter the power, presence, and love of God. Through teaching, practical exercises, and group ministry, participants learn to recognize God's voice, develop dynamic prayer and worship, and step into the biblical practices of healing and prophecy that marked the early church.

Available at Amazon.com

www.encounterdiscipleship.com

—

Visit **www.encounterpress.com** for more resources.

www.ingramcontent.com/pod-product-compliance
Lightning Source LLC
Chambersburg PA
CBHW030819090426
42737CB00009B/788